Becoming a Woman of

Excellence

30TH
ANNIVERSARY EDITION

CYNTHIA HEALD

*Now, my daughter, do not fear. I will do for you
whatever you ask, for all my people in the city
know that you are a woman of excellence.*

Ruth 3:11

A NavPress resource published in alliance
with Tyndale House Publishers, Inc.

NavPress is the publishing ministry of The Navigators, an international Christian organization and leader in personal spiritual development. NavPress is committed to helping people grow spiritually and enjoy lives of meaning and hope through personal and group resources that are biblically rooted, culturally relevant, and highly practical.

For more information, visit www.NavPress.com.

Becoming a Woman of Excellence 30th Anniversary Edition

Copyright © 1987, 1999, 2005, 2010, 2016 by Cynthia Heald. All rights reserved.

A NavPress resource published in alliance with Tyndale House Publishers, Inc.

Visit the author's website at www.cynthiaheald.com.

NAVPRESS and the NAVPRESS logo are registered trademarks of NavPress, The Navigators, Colorado Springs, CO. *TYNDALE* is a registered trademark of Tyndale House Publishers, Inc. Absence of ® in connection with marks of NavPress or other parties does not indicate an absence of registration of those marks.

Cover vintage border copyright © Vintage Style Designs/Creative Market. All rights reserved.
Cover typeface and floral illustration copyright © Lisa Glanz/Creative Market. All rights reserved.
Cover font by Laura Worthington/Creative Market. All rights reserved.
Author photo by Shelly Han Photography, copyright © 2016. All rights reserved.

The Team:
Don Pape, Publisher
Caitlyn Carlson, Acquiring Editor
Lynn Vanderzalm, Editor
Jennifer Ghionzoli, Designer

Unless otherwise indicated, all Scripture quotations are taken from the New American Standard Bible,® copyright © 1960, 1962, 1963, 1968, 1971, 1972, 1973, 1975, 1977, 1995 by The Lockman Foundation. Used by permission. Scripture quotations marked AMPC are taken from the *Amplified Bible,*® Classic Edition, copyright © 1954, 1958, 1962, 1964, 1965, 1987 by The Lockman Foundation. Used by permission. Scripture quotations marked KJV are taken from the *Holy Bible,* King James Version. Scripture quotations marked MSG are taken from *THE MESSAGE* by Eugene H. Peterson, copyright © 1993, 1994, 1995, 1996, 2000, 2001, 2002. Used by permission of NavPress Publishing Group. All rights reserved. Scripture quotations marked NIV are taken from the Holy Bible, *New International Version,*® *NIV.*® Copyright © 1973, 1978, 1984, 2011 by Biblica, Inc.® Used by permission. All rights reserved worldwide. Scripture quotations marked NLT are taken from the *Holy Bible,* New Living Translation, copyright © 1996, 2004, 2015 by Tyndale House Foundation. Used by permission of Tyndale House Publishers, Inc., Carol Stream, Illinois 60188. All rights reserved. Scripture verses marked *Phillips* are taken from *The New Testament in Modern English* by J. B. Phillips, copyright © J. B. Phillips, 1958, 1959, 1960, 1972. All rights reserved. Scripture quotations marked TLB are taken from *The Living Bible,* copyright © 1971 by Tyndale House Foundation. Used by permission of Tyndale House Publishers, Inc., Carol Stream, Illinois 60188. All rights reserved. Scripture quotations marked (Wuest) are taken from *The New Testament: An Expanded Translation,* Kenneth S. Wuest (Wuest), copyright © 1961, Wm. B. Eerdmans Publishing Company. Used by permission. All rights reserved.

Some of the anecdotal illustrations in this book are true to life and are included with the permission of the persons involved. All other illustrations are composites of real situations, and any resemblance to people living or dead is purely coincidental.

Library of Congress Cataloging-in-Publication Data

Names: Heald, Cynthia, author.
Title: Becoming a woman of excellence / Cynthia Heald.
Description: 30th Anniversary Edition. | Colorado Springs : NavPress, 2016. | Includes bibliographical references.
Identifiers: LCCN 2016015627 (print) | LCCN 2016016498 (ebook) | ISBN 9781631465642 | ISBN 9781631465673 (Apple) | ISBN 9781631465659(E-Pub) | ISBN 9781631465666 (Kindle)
Subjects: LCSH: Christian women—Religious life—Textbooks. | Excellence—Religious aspects—Christianity—Textbooks.
Classification: LCC BV4527 .H3978 2016 (print) | LCC BV4527 (ebook) | DDC 248.8/43—dc23LC record available at https://lccn.loc.gov/2016015627

Printed in the United States of America

22   21   20   19   18   17   16

7   6   5   4   3   2   1

the Father spoke:

Come, child, let us journey together.

Where shall we go, Father?

To a distant land, another Kingdom.

So the journey will be long?

Yes, we must travel every day.

When will we reach our destination?

At the end of your days.

And who will accompany us?

Joy and Sorrow.

Must Sorrow travel with us?

Yes, she is necessary to keep you close to Me.

But I want only Joy.

It is only with Sorrow that you will know true Joy.

What must I bring?

A willing heart to follow Me.

What shall I do on the journey?

There is only one thing that you must do—stay close to Me.
  Let nothing distract you. Always keep your eyes on Me.

And what will I see?

You will see My glory.

And what will I know?

You will know My heart.

The Father stretched out His hand. The child, knowing the great love her Father had for her, placed her hand in His, and they began their journey.

As a young woman, the Lord spoke these words to my heart. Ever since this conversation, my goal has been to keep my hand in His and to become a woman of excellence who brings honor to His name.

As you begin this journey, my prayer is that you will bring a willing heart, will firmly place your hand in His, and will become a woman of excellence who brings our Lord glory.

Blessings,
Cynthia Heald

Contents

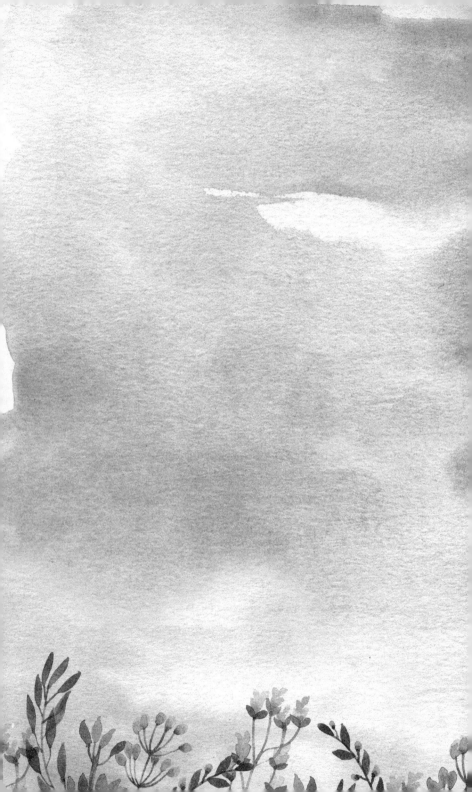

Preface

WHILE READING THROUGH THE BOOK of Ruth, I was struck with Boaz's praise of Ruth: "Now, my daughter, do not fear. I will do for you whatever you ask, for all my people in the city know that you are a woman of excellence" (Ruth 3:11).

My immediate response to this passage was to ask, "What made Ruth a woman of excellence?" As I studied her life, I discovered qualities that spoke strongly of strength and excellence. Through prayer and further Bible study, I learned that if we focus on developing and maintaining ourselves inwardly as God desires, then our responses and actions will follow accordingly.

As a result of my personal study, whenever I am confronted with choices or decisions, I find myself asking the question, "What would a woman of excellence do?" May this be your question, too, as we become women of excellence for the honor and glory of God.

Cynthia Heald

Preface

WHEN I WROTE the original preface for *Becoming a Woman of Excellence* thirty years ago, I had no idea that I would have an opportunity to revise this book. God has been gracious to keep His hand on this study—and me—so that I could share my journey of excellence as a certified older woman.

As I reflect on these past decades, I'm amazed that I continue to ask, "What would a woman of excellence do?" Using this question to determine my choices and setting my heart to "approve the things that are excellent" (Philippians 1:10) has served to guide and protect me in special ways. It is a priceless blessing to look back over my life and have few regrets.

One of the key verses in my life now is Psalm 71:18: "Now that I am old and gray, do not abandon me, O God. Let me proclaim your power to this new generation, your mighty miracles to all who come after me" (NLT). So it is with much thankfulness to God that I commit this study to all who come after me. May you discover the great joy of taking God at His word and walking with

Him daily in order to become a woman of excellence who brings Him honor and glory.

I am most grateful to be a small part of your life. May the Lord richly bless you as you deepen your intimacy with Him and study His Word.

Keep your hand in His,
Cynthia Heald

Suggestions

– FOR USING THIS STUDY –

BECOMING A WOMAN OF EXCELLENCE is suitable for group or individual study and for women of all ages, either married or single. If you desire to lead this study for a group, you will find a guide for Bible study leaders at the end of the book.

Each chapter includes personal thoughts and reflections from the author. Use these thoughts to prompt your examination and application of the study to your own life.

Most of the questions lead you into the Bible to help you base your responses on the Word of God. Let the Scriptures speak to you personally; there is not always a right or wrong answer.

Each chapter begins with a foundational Scripture passage for you to memorize. You may memorize the verse before or after doing the chapter study, in any Bible translation you choose. Write the memory verses (from your favorite version) on a card or Post-it, put it in a place where you will see it regularly, and memorize it. Thank God for who He is and for what He is doing in your life.

A dictionary and any Bible references or commentaries can be good resources for you in answering the questions. You'll also find them helpful in any further Bible study you might do on your own.

PART ONE

the Goal

CHAPTER 1

Excellence:

A GOAL WORTH PURSUING

This I pray, that your love may abound still more and more in real knowledge and all discernment, so that you may approve the things that are excellent, in order to be sincere and blameless until the day of Christ.

PHILIPPIANS 1:9-10

ONE DAY WHILE READING THE OLD TESTAMENT book of Ruth, I was touched by the words that Boaz spoke to Ruth: "All my people in the city know that you are a woman of excellence" (Ruth 3:11).

The description surprised me. I had always thought that *excellence* indicated success or high achievement or perfection. But here the word was used to describe a woman who was destitute. Ruth was a widow, a foreigner, and her life was what we would consider hand-to-mouth. She provided for herself and her mother-in-law by working in the fields, gleaning the grain that the harvesters missed.

So what was it about Ruth that made Boaz describe her as a woman of excellence?

If we look at the whole story, we learn that Ruth was the

daughter-in-law of Elimelech and Naomi. When a severe famine struck the land of Israel, Elimelech and his family moved from their hometown of Bethlehem to nearby Moab, where the sons married Moabite women, Orpah and Ruth. After a number of years, Elimelech and both of his sons died. When Naomi heard that the famine was over in Judah, she decided to return to her home. She encouraged her daughters-in-law to stay in Moab with their families, but Ruth loved Naomi and Naomi's God and chose instead to go with her mother-in-law, despite the fact that Naomi was heartbroken and downcast.

After arriving in Bethlehem, Ruth gleaned in the fields of Elimelech's relative Boaz, who greeted her as she worked. He had heard that she had refused to stay in her homeland because she was committed to her mother-in-law, and he was impressed by her loyalty.

He also knew that other people in the town considered her a virtuous woman, a woman of noble character. Ruth's selflessness in "approving the things that are excellent" earned her the reputation of being a woman of excellence, of strength, and of worth.

❧ THE SEARCH FOR EXCELLENCE

1. Most people define *excellence* as the quality of being very good at something, being the highest and the best, something that is superior, or the quality of being virtuous. What words or thoughts would you add to those definitions of *excellence*?

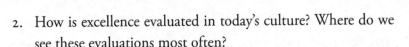
2. How is excellence evaluated in today's culture? Where do we see these evaluations most often?

3. How does the Christian community define and measure excellence?

The church is in almost as much trouble as the culture, for the church has bought into the same value system: fame, success, materialism, and celebrity. We watch the leading churches and the leading Christians for our cues.[1]

CHARLES COLSON

BIBLICAL VIEW OF EXCELLENCE

The word translated "excellent" in the New Testament comes from the Greek word *diapherō*, which literally means "to transport" or "to differ." Scripture translations also render the word as "best," "vital," "the better things," or "the highest and best."

The Hebrew word translated "excel" in Proverbs 31:29 is *alah*, which means "to ascend."

Both of these words are used to encourage us to ascend, to transport or to carry above the norm, to be different through the qualities of virtue and goodness.

4. Our culture tends to honor wealth, talent, beauty, success, and achievement. What are the qualities the following verses suggest we should cultivate in order to please God?

ROMANS 12:1-2

JAMES 1:27

1 JOHN 2:15-17

5. The following three Scripture passages give a biblical view of excellence and suggest a number of possible synonyms for the concept of excellence. Read each passage and record your thoughts about how these amplifications help, whether you are single or married, in your understanding of excellence.

RUTH 3:11 (AMPC)—*All my people in the city know that you are a woman of strength (worth, bravery, capability).*

PROVERBS 12:4 (AMPC)—*A virtuous and worthy wife [earnest and strong in character] is a crowning joy to her husband.*

PROVERBS 31:10 (AMPC)—*A capable, intelligent, and virtuous woman—who is he who can find her?*

My thoughts on the meaning and manifestation of excellence:

6. What do the following verses teach about our pursuit of the "highest and best" and how we can "approve the things that are excellent"?

1 CORINTHIANS 10:31 ······································

PHILIPPIANS 1:9-10 ·· ✷

PHILIPPIANS 4:8 ··· ✷

7. If the goal of our pursuit of excellence is not clear, we risk losing sight of what it is we're pursuing or desiring. The following Scripture passages give specific guidelines for how we should pursue growth and excellence in our walk with God. What does each passage tell us to do?

MATTHEW 22:36-39 ··· ✷

2 TIMOTHY 2:15 ·· ✷

2 PETER 1:3-8, especially verses 5-7 ··················· ✷

8. From the verses you've studied so far, how would you explain the biblical view of excellence to a friend?

 ## THOUGHTS AND REFLECTIONS FROM AN OLDER WOMAN

When I was a young girl, my mother told me many times, "If you are going to do anything, do it right!" This admonition was applied to everything from setting the table, to ironing a dress, to washing the dishes. My mom did not expect perfection, but her thought was that if I were to undertake a task, then I should do it to the best of my ability. I didn't realize it then, but early in my life I was being taught the value of excellence—of doing things well.

The year I celebrated my fortieth birthday was a pivotal one for me. The forty years had passed so quickly, and I realized that my life was probably half over! I reflected on my past—accepting Christ, graduating from college, marrying Jack, teaching English, and moving several times. I recalled the cooking, the cleaning, and the carpooling for four children. I concluded that my life was blessed and full and that I was right where I needed to be.

But I also realized that somewhere over the years, I had settled for a goal of mediocrity. I could identify with the secretary who had this sign over her desk: "Today I think I'll try to accomplish something . . . like getting through it!" So at that stage in my life, I decided I wanted to embrace all that God might have for me in my remaining years.

As I read through the Scriptures that year with this new perspective, I was impressed and moved by Boaz's comment to Ruth about her excellence. I immediately realized that when she had decided to go and serve Naomi, she trusted God with her life. Ruth was not allowing her circumstances to dictate her behavior or responses. Commentator David Atkinson said this about Ruth's decision: "At the centre of this expression of love and commitment to Naomi—in journeying, in home, in family, in life and in death—is a commitment to share Naomi's God."[2]

When Boaz first encountered Ruth, he blessed her by saying, "May the LORD, the God of Israel, under whose wings you have come to take refuge, reward you fully for what you have done" (Ruth 2:12, NLT). I feel that Ruth's goal was to seek first the Kingdom of God—something she could not do in Moab and something for which she was willing to sacrifice.

As I contemplated the qualities that produced her noble character, I silently prayed, *Lord, I don't know how many years I have left, but I don't want to miss out on anything You have for me. For the rest of my life I want to be in the process of loving You with all my heart, soul, and mind, seeking first your Kingdom, and approving the things that are excellent in order to become a woman of excellence—for Your glory.*

After this prayer of commitment, I decided that as much as possible, whenever I was faced with a choice or a response, I would ask myself, *What would a woman of excellence do?* or *How would a woman of excellence respond?* I encourage you to keep these questions in the forefront of your thinking, for they have been a great help in my daily pursuit of embracing excellence as a lifestyle.

PERSONAL THOUGHTS AND REFLECTIONS

9. Take a few minutes to reflect on your own life. How were you encouraged to excel? Were these ways a help or a hindrance to your understanding of excellence? Write your thoughts.

10. Read the following Scripture passages, and write about the one important truth you need to grasp in order to have God's best for your life.

MATTHEW 6:33 ....

PHILIPPIANS 3:12-14 ....

HEBREWS 6:1 ....

Throughout our study we will explore not only God's call to excellence but also His provision, patience, and assurance that His power is perfected in weakness. From the beginning we need to realize that excellence is not perfection, but essentially a desire to be strong *in* the Lord and *for* the Lord. Oswald Chambers gave this perspective on excellence: "We have to realise that no effort can be too high, because Jesus says we are to be the children of our Father in heaven. It must be my utmost for His highest all the time and every time."[3]

11. Review this chapter and record any insights that were especially meaningful to you in learning to become a woman of excellence. After thinking over the Scripture passages you've read, write down a goal you'd like to set for yourself in doing this study. A possible goal might be, "To understand how I can become a woman of excellence." The apostle Paul expressed one of his goals in 2 Corinthians 5:9: "Whether we are here in this body or away from this body, our goal is to please him" (NLT). Establishing a goal will help remind you of your purpose and commitment as you work through the study.

MY GOAL:

A HEART FOR GOD'S WORD

Scripture memory enables us to remember our goals and to open our hearts to the transforming work of the Holy Spirit. The psalmist David wrote, "I take joy in doing your will, my God, for your instructions are written on my heart" (Psalm 40:8, NLT). Having God's Word in our hearts spurs us on to obey and to grow.

I know of no other single practice in the Christian life more rewarding, practically speaking, than memorizing Scripture. That's right. No other single discipline is more useful and rewarding than this. No other single exercise pays greater spiritual dividends! Your prayer life will be strengthened. . . . Your attitudes and outlook will begin to change. Your mind will become alert and observant. Your confidence and assurance will be enhanced. Your faith will be solidified.[4]

CHARLES R. SWINDOLL

SCRIPTURE MEMORY

PHILIPPIANS 1:9-10—*This I pray, that your love may abound still more and more in real knowledge and all discernment, so that you may approve the things that are excellent, in order to be sincere and blameless until the day of Christ.*

CHAPTER 2

Excellence:

GOD'S CHARACTER

The LORD is my light and my salvation; whom shall I fear? The LORD is the defense of my life; whom shall I dread?

PSALM 27:1

IF WE ARE GOING TO pursue a life goal that reflects our desire to "be our utmost for His highest," then we need to study God's character—for He is not only the source of excellence but also our model for excellence. We want to become women of excellence because we are children of an excellent God.

To begin the journey of becoming a woman of excellence, we must realize that we cannot reach this goal on our own merit or in our own strength. Because we are not perfect, it's good for us to examine God's character to see how He responds to our imperfections and weaknesses.

First, we need to acknowledge God's lovingkindness—reflected in His unfailing, unconditional love as well as His all-sufficient grace. Second, we must recognize God's sovereignty—His loving control over all of life. Third, we need to accept God's loving provision for us, giving us everything we need to do His will. Even though God is the all-powerful Creator, He cares about each of us individually. The psalmist wrote very personally that God is *my* light, *my* salvation, and *my* defense.

As we study these three major attributes of God's character, may we continue to be challenged to live a life reflecting His excellence.

We must practice the art of long and loving meditation upon the majesty of God. This will take some effort, for the concept of majesty has all but disappeared from the human race.[1]

A. W. TOZER

GOD'S LOVINGKINDNESS

How excellent is thy lovingkindness.

PSALM 36:7, KJV

1. A. W. Tozer wrote, "The divine attributes are what we know to be true of God."[2] What words would you use to describe God's character?

2. Read the rich descriptions of God's attributes in the following passages. List the attributes, then place a star near the aspects of God's personhood for which you are most thankful.

PSALM 103:8-14 ....

PSALM 145:8-20 ....

3. Sometimes our view of God is shaped by our human relationships. For example, if you were brought up in a very strict, harsh home or with other rigid authority figures, then you might see God primarily as a judge. But the Scriptures describe Him as loving and kind. Truly believing in God's lovingkindness is key to any response we have to Him.

Which characteristics of God, if any, do you find most difficult to accept because of your past experiences?

Which characteristics have blessed and encouraged your faith?

Write a brief prayer expressing either praise for who God is or your need for God to give you a fuller understanding of who He really is.

4. Alexander Maclaren commented, "God's love is not drawn out by our lovableness, but wells up, like an artesian spring, from the depths of his nature."[3] What do the following passages teach about the kind of love and grace God has for you?

PSALM 63:3 ··

ROMANS 5:8 ··

EPHESIANS 1:3-8 ···

1 JOHN 4:9-10 ···

5. How does accepting God's unconditional, unfailing love for you as His child strengthen your trust in Him?

Beloved, let us love.
Lord, what is love?
Love is that which inspired My life, and led Me to My
*   Cross, and held Me on My cross. Love is that which will*
*   make it thy joy to lay down thy life for thy brethren.*
Lord, evermore give me this love.
Blessed are they which do hunger and thirst after love,
*   for they shall be filled.[4]*

AMY CARMICHAEL

❧ GOD'S SOVEREIGNTY

Praise Him according to His excellent greatness.

PSALM 150:2

Sovereignty means supreme power, rule, authority, supremacy.

───────────── ∾ ─────────────

God's sovereignty is the attribute by which He rules His entire creation, and to be sovereign God must be all-knowing, all-powerful, and absolutely free . . . to do whatever He wills to do anywhere at any time to carry out His eternal purpose in every single detail without interference.[5]

A. W. TOZER

6. What do you learn about God's sovereignty from the following verses?

1 CHRONICLES 29:11-12 ·· ∾

PSALM 115:3 ··· ∾

ISAIAH 46:9-10 ....

COLOSSIANS 1:15-17 ....

7. God's lovingkindness and rule are evident in the following verses. What do you learn about His sovereign care for you?

JEREMIAH 29:11 ....

JOHN 16:33 ....

ROMANS 8:28 ....

What assurance and comfort do these verses give you as you face the trials and sorrows of life?

8. Whether we are Christians or not, we will all face trials in life. The difference in the Christian's life is that God's grace is sufficient to help us triumph through them and bear up under them. Study the following passages about suffering: Psalm 119:71; John 9:1-3; 2 Corinthians 4:7-10; 2 Corinthians 12:7-10. How would you explain the Bible's view of suffering?

No literature is more realistic and honest in facing the harsh facts of life than the Bible. At no time is there the faintest suggestion that the life of faith exempts us from difficulties. What it promises is preservation from all the evil in them. . . . All the water in all the oceans cannot sink a ship unless it gets inside. Nor can all the trouble in the world harm us unless it gets within us. That is the promise of [Psalm 121]: "GOD guards you from every evil."[6]

EUGENE PETERSON

9. We also need to recognize the role we play in many of our trials. Sometimes the difficulties are the result of the willfulness of our own sinful nature. What do the following Scripture passages teach about our human role in bringing trials on ourselves? As you read the passages, think about your own heart.

    PSALM 81:8-14 ··

    JEREMIAH 7:23-24 ···

    MATTHEW 7:24-27 ··

10. Someone has said that God is a gentleman, and He will not force His will on us; we must give Him permission to rule in our lives. If this is your desire, write a prayer giving God permission to rule in your heart.

———————— ⟨⟩ ————————

To believe actively that our Heavenly Father constantly
spreads around us providential circumstances that work for
our present good and our everlasting well-being brings to
the soul a veritable benediction. Most of us go through life
praying a little, planning a little, jockeying for position,
hoping but never being quite certain of anything, and
always secretly afraid that we will miss the way. This is a
tragic waste of truth and never gives rest to the heart.
There is a better way. It is to repudiate our own wisdom
and take instead the infinite wisdom of God. Our insistence
upon seeing ahead is natural enough, but it is a real
hindrance to our spiritual progress. God has charged Himself
with full responsibility for our eternal happiness and stands
ready to take over the management of our lives the moment
we turn in faith to Him.[7]

A. W. TOZER

GOD'S PROVISION

Praise the LORD in song, for He has done excellent
things.

ISAIAH 12:5

11. The psalmist David used his own experience of being a
    shepherd to write the beautiful twenty-third psalm. Read
    Psalm 23 and Matthew 6:31-33. List the ways the divine
    shepherd cares for you, His precious sheep.

How does experiencing God's personal care and provision encourage and expand your view of God?

When the Lord is my Shepherd he is able to supply my needs, and he is certainly willing to do so, for his heart is full of love, and therefore "I shall not want." I shall not lack for temporal things. Does he not feed the ravens, and cause the lilies to grow? How, then, can he leave his children to starve? I shall not want for spirituals, I know that his grace will be sufficient for me. Resting in him he will say to me, "As thy day so shall thy strength be."[8]

C. H. SPURGEON

12. Since the Lord is our defense, what do you learn from the following passages about how God meets your needs for security and protection?

PSALM 27:1 ·

PSALM 91:4, 14-16 ·

ROMANS 8:31-32 ·· ᧐

1 PETER 1:3-5 ··· ᧐

————————— ᧐ᑎ᧐ —————————

Be assured, if you walk with Him and look to Him and expect help from Him, He will never fail you. An older brother who has known the Lord for forty-four years, who writes this, says to you for your encouragement that He has never failed him. In the greatest difficulties, in the heaviest trials, in the deepest poverty and necessities, He has never failed me; but because I was enabled by His grace to trust Him, He has always appeared for my help. I delight in speaking well of His name."[9]

GEORGE MUELLER

🌿 THOUGHTS AND REFLECTIONS FROM AN OLDER WOMAN

Early in my life I responded to God's love for me. Knowing that God loves me unconditionally has freed me from trying to live the Christian life by being perfect and trying to earn His love by performing. Because of my security and worth in Jesus Christ, I do not have to look to people or things to feel valued or loved. I am now free to love and serve because I can trust my needs to be met by my heavenly Father.

My understanding of God's constancy in His love encourages me to return His love by living a life that would honor Him. I want to become a woman of excellence—not because I have to perform, but because I choose to please God. My continuing goal is to be His child, a child who has a strong family resemblance to her Father—who is excellent in every facet of His nature.

Now that I am in my seventh decade, I can heartily concur with George Mueller's affirmation of God's faithfulness. Although I have failed God, He has never failed me. He is a loving, gracious, giving, protective Father, and my constant prayer is that I will always be in the process of becoming a woman of excellence, reflecting His character by being loving and gracious wherever He places me. I, too, delight in speaking well of His name.

PERSONAL THOUGHTS AND REFLECTIONS

13. Psalm 145:17 declares, "The LORD is righteous in all His ways and kind in all His deeds." As you review this chapter, what aspect of God's character has challenged or encouraged you? Why?

How can this part of God's character make a difference in your life as you begin your journey of becoming a woman of excellence?

Look back over your own history as revealed to you by grace, and you will see one central fact growing large— God is love. . . . In the future, when trial and difficulties await you, do not be fearful; whatever and whoever you may lose faith in, let not this faith slip from you—God is Love.[10]

OSWALD CHAMBERS

SCRIPTURE MEMORY

PSALM 27:1—*The LORD is my light and my salvation; whom shall I fear? The LORD is the defense of my life; whom shall I dread?*

CHAPTER 3

Excellence:

BECOMING LIKE CHRIST

All of us who have had that veil removed can see and reflect the glory of the Lord. And the Lord—who is the Spirit—makes us more and more like him as we are changed into his glorious image.

2 CORINTHIANS 3:18, NLT

A MAJOR FACET of God's love for us is expressed in His desire for us to grow—to become like His Son, Christ. Eugene Peterson's paraphrase of Romans 8:29 says, "God knew what he was doing from the very beginning. He decided from the outset to shape the lives of those who love him along the same lines as the life of his Son" (MSG).

Our desire for excellence and for becoming women who bring God glory delights Him, but we must understand that His purpose is to conform us to the image of Christ. This transformation is a lifelong journey. Growth occurs when we maintain our walk with God—remembering that the Christian life is a *process*.

To *become* means to grow into, to come to be, to undergo change or development, to be transformed. As we choose to consistently abide in Christ, we are made more and more like Him and changed into His glorious image.

*There is a great market for religious experience in our world;
there is little enthusiasm for the patient acquisition of virtue,
little inclination to sign up for a long apprenticeship in what
earlier generations of Christians called holiness.*[1]

EUGENE PETERSON

❧ GOD'S DESIRE FOR US

1. In Psalm 103:8 the psalmist proclaims that God abounds in lovingkindness and unfailing love. What do you learn in the following passages about God's desire to be in relationship to you?

   PSALM 149:4

   JEREMIAH 29:13

   MATTHEW 11:28-30

EPHESIANS 2:4-7 ···

How do these verses encourage you to seek God's presence and work in your life?

2. Another word for *becoming like Christ* is *sanctification*. To "sanctify" means to "make holy." Sanctification is growing in divine grace as a result of Christian commitment. Oswald Chambers provided this thought: "Sanctification means being made one with Jesus so that the disposition that ruled in Him will rule us."[2] What do you learn from the following verses about the process of becoming like Christ?

ROMANS 8:28-29 ···

2 CORINTHIANS 3:16-18 ································

PHILIPPIANS 1:6 ·· ↝

PHILIPPIANS 2:13 ··· ↝

In order to avoid discouragement and reliance on ourselves, it is important to know that God has begun His work in us and He will complete it. But how encouraging to realize also that God is patient with the process! Oswald Chambers challenged us, "It takes a long time to realise what Jesus is after, and the person you need most patience with is yourself. God takes deliberate time with us; He does not hurry, because we can only appreciate His point of view by a long discipline."[3]

When we are tempted to be impatient with the process, we need to remember that Joseph was in prison approximately nine years before Pharaoh called him out to interpret a dream and put him in charge of the Egyptian kingdom. The apostle Paul was in Arabia several years before going on his first missionary journey. We should also remember that God's view of time is different from ours. The apostle Peter reminds us, "Do not let this one fact escape your notice, beloved, that with the Lord one day is like a thousand years, and a thousand years like one day" (2 Peter 3:8).

3. In Philippians 3:12-14 the apostle Paul made it clear that he was still "in process." According to these verses, what was Paul's plan to keep on growing?

During the life of Jesus on earth, the word He chiefly used when speaking of the relations of the disciples to Himself was: "Follow me." When about to leave for heaven, He gave them a new word, in which their more intimate and spiritual union with Himself in glory should be expressed. That chosen word was: "Abide in me."[4]

ANDREW MURRAY

4. In the upper room, Jesus shared with His disciples the blessings of abiding—of staying connected to Him. Carefully read John 15:1-11; then answer the following questions:

What are the key words in this passage?

What does it mean to "abide" or "remain"?

What are the benefits of abiding or remaining in Christ?

What are the results of *not* abiding or remaining in Christ?

What is one way of knowing that we are abiding or remaining in Christ?

———————————— ⟳ ————————————

*It needs time to grow into Jesus the Vine: do not expect
to abide in Him unless you will give Him that time. . . .
Come, my brethren, and let us day by day set ourselves
at His feet, and meditate on this word of His, with an
eye fixed on Him alone. Let us set ourselves in quiet trust
before Him, waiting to hear His holy voice—the still
small voice that is mightier than the storm that rends the
rocks—breathing its quickening spirit within us, as He
speaks: "Abide in Me."[5]*

ANDREW MURRAY

5. To abide in Christ is to stay in living contact with Him. What do you learn from the following verses about how you can abide in or remain in Jesus?

JOHN 8:31 ⟶

2 TIMOTHY 3:16 ⟶

The Scriptures were given not to increase our knowledge, but to change our lives.[6]

DWIGHT L. MOODY

OUR DESIRE FOR GOD

Prayer—secret, fervent, believing prayer—lies at the root of all personal godliness.[7]

WILLIAM CAREY

6. Charles Spurgeon once said, "Holy desires are among the most powerful influences that stir our inner nature."[8]

Read and reflect on the following Scripture passages. Write down the imagery that is used to describe desire for God.

PSALM 42:1-2 .... ✑

PSALM 63:1 .... ✑

PSALM 84:1-2 .... ✑

The authors of these psalms used passionate words: *longing, faint with longing, yearn, thirst,* and *cry out* to express their eagerness for the Lord. Why do you think the psalmists felt so strongly in their desire for God?

7. We could define meditation as prayerful reflection on the Word of God with a goal of understanding and applying it. What benefits of meditation does Psalm 1:1-3 claim?

What are some possible ways you can meditate on God's Word day and night?

❋ THOUGHTS AND REFLECTIONS FROM AN OLDER WOMAN

Although it was years ago, I still remember the time that Jesus' words in John 15:5 penetrated my heart. He spoke on the importance of abiding in order to bear fruit and ended with these words: "Apart from Me you can do nothing."

This pronouncement astonished me. I thought, *I don't want to come to the end of my life and realize that I have done nothing for His Kingdom, so if it takes abiding in Christ to bear fruit and to accomplish what He has planned for me, then I want to spend the rest of my life abiding in Him.*

That was a special turning point in my life. Now for more than forty years, it has been my joy and my plan to "press on" (to push forward, to advance, to forge ahead) to know the Lord. So day by day I set myself at His feet, read His Word, and wait in quiet trust before Him in order to be made more and more like Him.

Even though I have been abiding in the Lord for many years, I am still in process. You can ask my husband! Some of my continuing struggles are with taming my tongue, having self-control, and being patient. I have had some measure of victory in these areas, but I think Paul's words, as paraphrased in *The Message*, perfectly describe my heart:

> *I'm not saying that I have this all together, that I have it made. But I am well on my way, reaching out for Christ, who has so wondrously reached out for me. Friends, don't get me wrong: By no means do I count myself an expert in all of this, but I've got my eye on the goal, where God is beckoning us onward—to Jesus. I'm off and running, and I'm not turning back.*
>
> PHILIPPIANS 3:12-14

Or as a dear old saint once said, "I ain't what I ought to be, but I ain't what I used to be either!"

❧ PERSONAL THOUGHTS AND REFLECTIONS

8. In Psalm 18, David declared, "For who is God, but the LORD? And who is a rock, except our God, the God who girds me with strength and makes my way blameless?" (Psalm 18:31-32). Looking back over this chapter, take time to summarize the ways that God works in transforming you into the image of His Son.

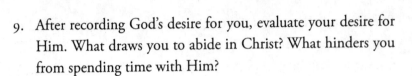

9. After recording God's desire for you, evaluate your desire for Him. What draws you to abide in Christ? What hinders you from spending time with Him?

10. Take a few minutes to write a psalm or prayer that expresses your longing to become conformed to the image of Christ.

There is only one relationship that matters, and that is your personal relationship to a personal Redeemer and Lord. Let everything else go, but maintain that at all costs, and God will fulfill His purpose through your life.[9]

OSWALD CHAMBERS

SCRIPTURE MEMORY

2 CORINTHIANS 3:18—*All of us who have had that veil removed can see and reflect the glory of the Lord. And the Lord—who is the Spirit—makes us more and more like him as we are changed into his glorious image.* (NLT)

Special note: In order to pattern our lives after Jesus, we need to first enter into a relationship with Him so that we can live in His strength—not our own. If you have never made the life-changing decision of inviting Jesus Christ to be your Savior and Lord, prayerfully consider the following verses, and speak to a friend or pastor who could help you in understanding your relationship to Christ.

> John 11:25-27
> John 14:6
> Romans 3:23
> Romans 6:23
> Romans 10:9-13

The following booklets can help you in relating to and growing in Christ:

> "Steps to Peace with God" (Billy Graham Evangelistic Association)[10]
> "The Bridge to Life Illustration" (NavPress)[11]
> "Seven Minutes with God" (NavPress)[12]
> *Lessons on Assurance* (NavPress)
> *The Quiet Time* (InterVarsity)

PART TWO

the Cost

CHAPTER 4

Excellence:

ROOTED IN SURRENDER

I have been crucified with Christ; and it is no longer I who live, but Christ lives in me; and the life which I now live in the flesh I live by faith in the Son of God, who loved me and gave Himself up for me.

GALATIANS 2:20

THE MORE TIME WE SPEND with God, praying and meditating on His Word, the more we find our focus in life changing from self-centeredness to Christ-centeredness. John the Baptist summed up the process of becoming like Christ: "He must become greater and greater, and I must become less and less" (John 3:30, NLT). The French theologian François Fénelon expressed the same thought: "Whatever spiritual knowledge or feelings we may have, they are all a delusion if they do not lead us to the real and constant practice of dying to self."[1] To die to self, or to surrender, means to give up, relinquish, yield, let go, abandon, submit, give up my rights.

Ruth, whose story we reflected on in chapter 1, epitomizes the essence of surrender. When Ruth's mother-in-law, Naomi, decided to return to her homeland, she made it very clear to her daughters-in-law, Ruth and Orpah, that there was no guarantee of their having a family or any kind of future in Bethlehem. Orpah chose to stay in Moab, but Ruth proclaimed her loyalty to Naomi with the beautiful words, "Where you go, I will go, and where you lodge, I will lodge. Your people shall be my people, and your God, my God" (Ruth 1:16). Ruth willingly gave up her rights and any desires or plans she had for her own life in order to know God more intimately and to serve Naomi. Ruth's life was rooted in surrender.

❦ "I MYSELF NO LONGER LIVE . . ."

There is only one thing God wants of us, and that is our unconditional surrender.[2]

OSWALD CHAMBERS

1. Jesus began His teaching on surrender by alluding to His impending sacrifice: "The hour has come for the Son of Man to be glorified" (John 12:23). In John 12:24-25, Jesus set forth some conditions and results related to our surrender before God. What are they?

2. Richard Foster defined self-denial as "simply a way of coming to understand that we do not have to have our own way."[3]

In Luke 9:23 Jesus outlined a three-point program for discipleship. Write a brief explanation of each point.

When Jesus mentioned self-denial and cross-bearing, what did he really mean? ([Mark 8:34]). Many think of self-denial as giving up something during the Lenten season. Others have said that it is to be dead to self or even to hate self. I disagree with these opinions. When Jesus referred to self-denial, he was not talking about denying ourselves some luxury item or denying the reality of self or the needs of self. Rather, he was focusing on the importance of renouncing self as the center of our life and actions. In other words, self-denial is the decision of each of his followers to give over to God his body, career, money, and time. A true disciple is willing to shift the spiritual center of gravity in his life. Self-denial is the sustained willingness to say no to oneself in order to say yes to God. . . . The cross . . . is the symbol of mission, essence of purpose. . . .Whatever mission God gives me is my cross.[4]

BILL HULL

3. In his letter to the Philippians, Paul wrote of his own personal surrender. Read Philippians 3:1-11. How does his example of

yielding his life challenge you? (In answering this question, it might help you to note not only *what* Paul surrendered but also *his purpose* for giving it up.)

You have trusted Him as your dying Saviour; now trust Him as your living Saviour. Just as much as He came to deliver you from future punishment, did He also come to deliver you from present bondage. Just as truly as He came to bear your stripes for you, has He come to live your life for you.[5]

HANNAH WHITALL SMITH

❧ "BUT CHRIST IS LIVING IN ME"

4. The Roman practice of crucifying criminals on a cross was an ever-present reminder of death during Paul's ministry. Read Colossians 3:1-4 and Galatians 2:20. How do these verses help you in your understanding of what it means to surrender?

————————— ⌒ —————————

The Spirit of God witnesses to the simple almighty security of the life hid with Christ in God.[6]

OSWALD CHAMBERS

5. Meditate on Paul's prayer in Ephesians 3:16-19. Write out the prayer, substituting the pronouns *I*, *me*, and *my* for the word *you*. Use this prayer often to renew your awareness of Christ's living in you.

6. In 1982, Lydia Joel was head of the dance department at the School of Performing Arts in New York City. In her lecture to freshman dancers, she said,

This is an absolutely undemocratic situation you face. You have no rights here. Your only right is to come to class and be wonderful. You can't protest, you can't be absent, you can only work. . . . You must give your entire self in an act of faith. If you have any sort of resentment or lack of clarity, you will find heartbreak. But if you manage to live through four years of this demand upon your inner self, your life will be literally changed.[7]

a. What were these students asked to give up?

b. What was their motivation for surrendering?

c. What was their reward?

7. If these dance students were willing to surrender to such demands to a secular institution, then how much more should we be willing to yield to Christ, who loves us and gave Himself for us? Consider and respond to these questions:

a. What does God ask of you? (See Matthew 10:37-39 and Luke 9:23, 14:27.)

b. What should be your motivation?

c. What are the rewards and benefits of your yielding?

d. It's comforting to understand that the process of relinquishing control is not always easy. What do you learn from the apostle Paul's struggles, as described in Romans 7:21-25?

In C. S. Lewis's book *The Screwtape Letters*, Screwtape (Satan) writes letters of instruction to his demon nephew, Wormwood, on how to keep a Christian from growing. Through this exchange, in which Screwtape explains to Wormwood the doctrine of surrender, Lewis highlighted a key result of God's grace in our lives:

> When He talks of their losing their selves, He means only abandoning the clamour of self-will; once they have done that, He really gives them back all their personality, and boasts (I am afraid, sincerely) that when they are wholly His, they will be more themselves than ever.[8]

8. In Romans 8:12-14, Paul summed up his discussion of living by the Spirit versus living according to our sinful nature. What did he tell us to do?

As we seek to become like Christ and learn to abide in the Vine, however, we begin to encounter some opposition. A. W. Tozer wrote, "It would seem that there is within each of us an enemy which we tolerate at our peril. Jesus called it 'life' and 'self,' or as we would say, the *self-life*. . . . To allow this enemy to live is in the end to lose everything. To repudiate it and give up all for Christ's sake is to lose nothing at last, but to preserve everything unto life eternal."[9]

⚘ THOUGHTS AND REFLECTIONS FROM AN OLDER WOMAN

When my husband, Jack, and I moved to a new town many years ago, we had three children all under the age of three. Jack was beginning his veterinary practice, and because he treated large and small animals, he was usually gone twelve to fourteen hours a day. Besides having three small children and an absent husband and father, we lived in a very old house that had mice! At the time I had no close friends—only One, who heard my cry: "Lord! I can't go on any more. I'm tired, I'm lonely. I want to give up."

Unmistakably, I heard God's voice in my heart: *Good. I don't want you to go on in your own strength. I want to live your life for you. I want you to know that when you relinquish control of your life, you can do all things because I strengthen you.* That was my initial surrendering. From that time on, I began to understand that the Christian life is not only *imitation*, but *habitation*. It's an exchanged life—His life for my life. Really, it's not an even exchange, as Elisabeth Elliot said: "What is ours belongs to Christ [and] what is His is ours."[10]

Since I'm still in the process of "becoming," I am continually challenged to surrender circumstances to Him daily. I appreciate Fénelon's phrase: the "constant practice of dying to self."[11]

For many years Galatians 2:20, which I quoted at the beginning of this chapter, has encouraged me to practice dependence on the Lord. It has been one of my favorite Scripture passages and one the Lord continues to use frequently to remind me that I no longer live, but that He lives in me. His presence guides me, comforts me, and gives me peace, hope, and the will to persevere.

How different Ruth's life would have been had she chosen to stay in Moab. She would not have grown in her faith, have married Boaz, or be named in the lineage of Christ. And how different my life would be if I had not abandoned it to God. I fear I would never have been startled by the description of Ruth as a woman of excellence and I would not have begun a wholehearted pursuit of living a life that would bring honor and glory to my Savior.

My surrendering has brought perspective and rest into my life, for now when I am overwhelmed by life's uncontrollable circumstances, the Lord will gently ask, *Cynthia, whose life is it?*

Because my life is rooted in surrender, it is with inexpressible joy I answer, "It's yours, Lord. It's yours."

George Mueller was known by people around the world for the extraordinary answers to his prayers on a continual basis. One day he was urged to share the secret of the effectiveness of his ministry and prayer life. In his answer he spoke of his "secret death." "There was a day," he said, "when I died; utterly died." He spoke deliberately and

*quietly, bending lower until he nearly touched the floor.
"I died to George Mueller, his opinions, preferences, tastes
and will; died to the world, its approval or censure; died
to the approval or blame even of my brethren and friends;
and since then I have studied only to show myself approved
of God."[12]*

❧ PERSONAL THOUGHTS AND REFLECTIONS

It's been said, "It's not how much we have of the Holy Spirit that matters, but how much the Holy Spirit has of us." The key is always submitting and abandoning ourselves to God. As Oswald Chambers said, "We have to keep letting go, and slowly and surely the great full life of God will invade us in every part, and men will take knowledge of us that we have been with Jesus."[13]

9. As you review this chapter, how have you been challenged to live your life rooted in surrender?

10. Have you surrendered your life to Christ? If so, describe your experience and the blessings you have gained in your dying to self.

If you have not abandoned your life to the Lord, would you prayerfully consider surrendering your life now? Hannah Whitall Smith's prayer may help you find the right words:

> Here, Lord, I abandon myself to thee. I have tried in every way I could think of to manage myself, and to make myself what I know I ought to be, but have always failed. Now I give it up to thee. Do thou take entire possession of me. Work in me all the good pleasure of thy will. Mould and fashion me into such a vessel as seemeth good to thee. I leave myself in thy hands, and I believe thou wilt, according to thy promise, make me into a vessel unto thy own honor, "sanctified, and meet for the master's use, and prepared unto every good work." [14]

 ## SCRIPTURE MEMORY

GALATIANS 2:20—*I have been crucified with Christ; and it is no longer I who live, but Christ lives in me; and the life which I now live in the flesh I live by faith in the Son of God, who loved me and gave Himself up for me.*

CHAPTER 5

Excellence:

EXEMPLIFIED BY OBEDIENCE

God is working in you, giving you the desire and the power to do what pleases him.

PHILIPPIANS 2:13, NLT

HANNAH WHITALL SMITH once said, "The life hid with Christ in God is a hidden life, as to its source, but it must not be hidden as to its practical results. People must see that we walk as Christ walked, if we say that we are abiding in Him. We must prove that we 'possess' that which we 'profess.'"[1] A one-word summary of her thoughts could be *obedience.*

Obedience is submission, habitually yielding to authority. The Greek word *hypakouō* is translated "to obey." It means to listen to, to answer. Jesus taught that a wise person hears and *acts.* How we listen to God and His Word determines our response.

The good news is that God's commands are not difficult to obey. The apostle John wrote this encouraging thought: "Loving God means keeping his commandments, and his commandments are not burdensome." (1 John 5:3, NLT) A godly saint observed, "Nothing is grievous or burdensome to him who loves. They are not grievous, because love makes them light; they are not grievous, because Christ gives strength to bear them."[2]

So obedience is not forced but should be motivated by a heart of love. David wrote in Psalm 40:8, "I take joy in doing your will, my God, for your instructions are written on my heart" (NLT). Puritan preacher and writer John Flavel commented, "Your delight and readiness in the paths of obedience is the very measure of your sanctification."[3]

If we have surrendered our lives to God, then we will naturally want to yield to His authority, to obey His commands, and to please Him by living His way.

❧ OBEYING FOR OUR GOOD

1. Read Deuteronomy 10:12-13, which summarizes some key aspects of the Christian life. What do these verses tell you about why you should keep or obey the Lord's commandments?

Oh that they had such a heart in them, that they would fear Me and keep all My commandments always, that it may be well with them and with their sons forever!

DEUTERONOMY 5:29

2. In Psalm 119 the psalmist expressed a wholehearted love for God's Word. What do the following verses tell you about the psalmist's attitudes toward God's commands?

PSALM 119:2-8 ·····································

PSALM 119:129 ·····································

PSALM 119:167 ·····································

3. Often I will be prompted by the Holy Spirit to call a friend, write a letter, or serve someone in a special way. I will respond

by thinking, *Yes, that's a good idea. I'll do that.* But then there are times I never get around to following through. Jesus taught about this particular attitude toward obedience. Read Luke 6:46-49 and write a brief paragraph summarizing His teaching on obedience.

What is the major lesson here for you?

In C. S. Lewis's *The Screwtape Letters*, Screwtape (Satan) instructs Wormwood on how to keep his Christian "patient" from obeying the Lord. Here is part of his letter: "Let him do anything but act. No amount of piety in his imagination and affections will harm us if we can keep it out of his will."[4] How very true that is!

4. Read Genesis 2:15-17 and 3:1-7, passages that tell the story of Adam and Eve's challenge to obey God's instructions. After reading these verses carefully, record your thoughts about the questions below.

a. What are the steps (strategy) Satan used to convince Eve that it was acceptable to disobey God's commands?

b. Why do you think Eve was so easily deceived, and what could she possibly have done to avoid Satan's deception? (To deceive means to cause to accept what is false, especially by trickery or misrepresentation.)[5]

c. Do you think it's possible that Eve felt God's command was not really for her good—because it *denied* her something, rather than promised to protect her? Why might she have felt this way?

d. Write down the similarities between Eve's progression to disobedience (Genesis 3:6) and the progression explained in James 1:13-15.

e. What can you learn about giving in to temptation from these verses?

5. From your study of Eve's disobedience and Satan's tactics, what insights have you gained to help you live a life that exemplifies obedience?

6. Another woman who struggled with obeying one of God's commands was Lot's wife. Read her story in Genesis 19:15-17 and 19:26. Why do you think she looked back?

What can you learn from her example and God's purpose in giving us commands?

⚜ OBEYING WITH HIS POWER

Our Lord never insists upon obedience; He tells us very emphatically what we ought to do, but He never takes means to make us do it. We have to obey Him out of a oneness of spirit.[6]

OSWALD CHAMBERS

7. It is our choice to obey or disobey God. His desire is that we voluntarily submit to Him. If we desire to yield to Him in what He has asked us to do, then we are not alone in our goal of obedience. How do these Scripture passages encourage us in our obedience?

ISAIAH 30:21 ···

PHILIPPIANS 2:13 ···

PHILIPPIANS 4:13 ···

Do I will to do the will of God? Then God will reinforce my will and enable me to do. Do I will to know the will of God? Then I will not take into consideration my own feelings and interests, "for even Christ pleased not Himself"—"never once consulted His own pleasure."[7]

AMY CARMICHAEL

8. One of the most powerful accounts of someone resisting Satan's temptations is that of Jesus' time in the wilderness. Read Matthew 4:1-11 and note how Jesus countered Satan's attempts to lead Him into evil.

9. Examine this chart, which parallels the temptation of Eve and the temptation of Jesus.[8]

Temptation	Genesis 3	Matthew 4
Appeal to the physical appetite	You may eat of any tree (3:1).	You may eat by changing stones to bread (4:3).
Appeal to personal gain	You will not die (3:4).	Angels will hold you up with their hands (4:6).
Appeal to power or glory	You will be like God (3:5).	You will have all the world's kingdoms (4:8-9).

a. What can you learn about Satan's tactics from this chart?

b. What can you do to strengthen the part of your life in which you feel most vulnerable?

Because everything which is in the world, the passionate desire of the flesh . . . and the passionate desire of the eyes, and the insolent and empty assurance which trusts in the things that serve the creature life, is not from the Father as a source but is from the world as a source. And the world is being caused to pass away, and its passionate desire. But the one who keeps on habitually doing the will of God abides forever.

1 JOHN 2:16-17, WUEST

🌿 OBEYING FOR OUR GROWTH

God desires us to become like His Son. We find in Scripture that Jesus "learned obedience from the things which He suffered" (Hebrews 5:8). Certainly one of the major ways that we learn obedience and grow strong in our faith is by persevering through trials. Jesus is our model; just as He was tempted and tried, so must we be challenged in the same way. How we respond to various tests reveals whether we have a heart to obey.

9. Paul beautifully illustrated the Lord's humility of heart in giving up His divine privileges. Read Philippians 2:5-8 and describe Jesus' attitude toward obedience.

This passage instructs us to have the same outlook as Christ did. What would that look like in specific areas of your life?

10. As you study the following verses, you might find this thought encouraging: "It is important to note that James did *not* say that a believer should be joyous *for* the trials but *in* the trials."[9] Read James 1:2-4 and 1 Peter 1:6-7.

What are the purposes of trouble and trials?

How should we respond to them?

11. Warren Wiersbe made this comment about trials: "No matter what the trials may be on the outside . . . or the temptations on the inside . . . through faith in Christ we can experience victory. The result of this victory is spiritual maturity."[10] What else do the following passages promise to those who learn obedience through suffering?

PSALM 119:71 ··

JAMES 1:12 ···

JAMES 5:11 ···

1 PETER 5:10 ··

---- ❧ ----

Your present circumstances that seem to be pressing so hard against you are the perfect tool in the Father's hand to chisel you into shape for eternity. So trust Him and never push away the instrument He is using, or you will miss the result of His work in your life.[11]

L. B. COWMAN

12. We could define obedience as willingly submitting to the process God has chosen for us to be conformed to the image of His Son. What trial are you currently facing? How can you begin to respond in a biblical way to this trial?

---- ❧ ----

The very best proof of your love for your Lord is obedience . . . nothing more, nothing less, nothing else.[12]

CHARLES R. SWINDOLL

❧ THOUGHTS AND REFLECTIONS FROM AN OLDER WOMAN

For me, obedience issues are related not so much to temptations to yield to evil as they are to struggles about doing what I should.

Procrastination, overcommitment to activities (often motivated by my desire for recognition), and not living my priorities are my battlefields in this area. James wrote, "Remember, it is sin to know what you ought to do and then not do it" (4:17, NLT). Most of my temptations and testings involve a choice to engage in activities that, although basically good in themselves, might come at the expense of my walk with God, my family, or other responsibilities. Just as Eve was deceived into thinking that she would become wise by eating the fruit, so I am often misled into making unwise decisions because the activity basically appeals to my flesh.

In the Old Testament we learn that the leader Joshua at one point entered into a covenant of peace with the Gibeonites—even though God had clearly instructed that Joshua should conquer them. Circumstances deceived Joshua and the elders, and Joshua 9:14 tells us that they "did not ask for the counsel of the LORD."

If only Eve had sought the counsel of God. If only I would take time to ask God's thoughts concerning my decisions. James wrote that if we lack wisdom when encountering trials and testings in our lives, we should ask God for direction: "If you need wisdom, ask our generous God, and he will give it to you. He will not rebuke you for asking" (1:5, NLT).

Although Joshua neglected to ask the Lord's counsel in regard to the Gibeonites, he responded differently when God instructed him to conquer Jericho. The night before the battle of Jericho, Joshua encountered a man with a sword standing in front of him, and when Joshua asked if he were friend or foe, the man answered that he was the commander of the Lord's army. "At this, Joshua fell with his face to the ground in reverence. 'I am at your command,' Joshua said. 'What do you want your servant to do?'" (Joshua 5:14, NLT).

Because I desire to exemplify obedience in my life, I have made Joshua's response my daily morning prayer: "Lord, I am at your command. What do you want me to do?"

Life, if true, should be always the offering up of what we are, to do our best for Him who has called us. . . . The true response is the result of a habit formed through the countless, nameless acts of conscientious obedience, which by use have become the bright and cheerful exercise of the one purpose of giving its best and purest to One most fully loved.[13]

THOMAS CARTER

PERSONAL THOUGHTS AND REFLECTIONS

Jesus said: "You are my friends if you obey me" (John 15:14, TLB).

As you look back over your study in this chapter, indicate any specific ways in which the Lord might be leading you to strengthen your obedience to Him, then write a prayer expressing your desire for your life to exemplify obedience.

SCRIPTURE MEMORY

PHILIPPIANS 2:13—*God is working in you, giving you the desire and the power to do what pleases him.* (NLT)

PART THREE

The Prize

CHAPTER 6

Excellence:

MOLDED BY DISCIPLINE

The Spirit God gave us does not make us timid, but gives us power, love and self-discipline.

2 TIMOTHY 1:7, NIV

IF WE DESIRE to become women of excellence, women who will become more and more like Christ in our behavior and character, then we need self-discipline.

Webster's Dictionary defines discipline as "training that corrects, molds, or perfects the mental faculties or moral character; orderly or prescribed conduct or pattern of behavior; self-control."[1]

Bible teacher Warren Wiersbe wrote that self-discipline "describes a person who is sensibly minded and balanced, who has [her] life under control."[2] Certainly, if our goal is to live to the glory of God, we must learn to control our desires and impulses.

It is comforting to know that we are not alone in the responsibility of acquiring self-discipline. As this chapter's verse reminds us, the Holy Spirit gives us power to practice self-discipline. As we abide in Christ and seek to obey Him, we will bear this precious fruit of the Spirit—self-control.

❦ THE NECESSITY OF DISCIPLINE

1. We can find many practical instructions for godly living in the book of Proverbs. Reflect on the following verses, and write why you think these proverbs are true.

   PROVERBS 16:32 ....

   PROVERBS 25:28 ....

2. Reflect on 2 Peter 1:2-8. Note that verses 2 and 3 speak of God's power, verse 4 about God's promises, and verses 5 through 8 about our response.

   What do you learn about God's power to help you?

What are God's promises to you?

What is your responsibility in the process of growing in faith?

"Add" [in 2 Peter 1:5] means there is something we have to do. We are in danger of forgetting that we cannot do what God does, and that God will not do what we can do. We cannot save ourselves nor sanctify ourselves, God does that; but God will not give us good habits, He will not give us character, He will not make us walk aright. We have to do all that ourselves; we have to work out the salvation God has worked in. "Add" means to get into the habit of doing things.[3]

OSWALD CHAMBERS

3. The following verses use different Greek words for the word *discipline*.[4] Read each verse, and in the third column write the English equivalent that your Bible translation uses.

References	Greek word used	English equivalent
Romans 12:3 2 Timothy 1:7	sōphroneō (to be of sound mind)	
Galatians 5:23 2 Peter 1:6	enkrateia (power over oneself)	
1 Timothy 4:7 Hebrews 5:14	gymnazō (train)	

We would do well to think of the Christian life as the path of disciplined Grace. It is discipline, because there is work for us to do. It is Grace, because the life of God which we enter into is a gift which we can never earn. Lovingly God works his life into us by Grace alone, joyfully we hammer out the reality of this new life on the anvil of discipline.

Remember, discipline in and of itself does not make us righteous; it merely places us before God. Having done this, discipline has reached the end of its tether. The transformation . . . is God's work.[5]

RICHARD FOSTER

DISCIPLINING THE MIND

4. Jesus taught that we should love God with all our heart, all our soul, and all our mind (Matthew 22:37). Study the

following verses and consider two things: what you are asked to do and why you think emphasis is placed on your mind and thoughts.

ISAIAH 26:3 ....

ROMANS 12:2 ....

2 CORINTHIANS 10:4-5 ....

COLOSSIANS 3:1-3 ....

5. Being controlled by the Holy Spirit is indispensable to living a life that pleases God. Read Romans 8:5-8. What do these verses say about the mind?

This passage [Romans 8:6-8] makes it abundantly clear that the way one thinks is intimately related to the way one lives, whether in Christ, in the Spirit and by faith, or alternatively in the flesh, in sin and in spiritual death.[6]

NEW INTERNATIONAL DICTIONARY OF NEW
TESTAMENT THEOLOGY

❧ DISCIPLINING THE WILL

It is sometimes thought that the emotions are the governing power in our nature. But I think we all of us know, as a matter of practical experience, that there is something within us, behind our emotions and behind our wishes, an independent self, that, after all, decides everything and controls everything. Our emotions belong to us, and are suffered and enjoyed by us, but they are not ourselves; and if God is to take possession of us, it must be into this central will or personality that He enters.[7]

HANNAH WHITALL SMITH

6. Our response to God should never be contingent on how we *feel*. From the following passages, write down the specific choices the psalmist made in exercising his will. Note the many times he said, "I will," especially in the first passage.

PSALM 101:1-4 ···

PSALM 119: 11, 15-16, 101 ·································

 DISCIPLINING OUR EMOTIONS

Christian psychologist Larry Crabb teaches that right thinking and right behavior lead to right feelings.[8] Our emotions are consequences of our thinking and actions. So it is important that we discipline our minds and wills. When we have been hurt or rejected, though, our emotions can overpower us, causing us to feel helpless. I have found it helpful to immediately acknowledge exactly how I feel to God. After I have let Him know my feelings, I am usually able to exercise my will and choose to think the truth. Often the truth I need to remind myself of is that God loves me and is for me and that He will guide me in doing what is needed and what is right.

7. One of the best ways of handling our emotions is fully acknowledging our feelings to God. Read Psalm 55. David felt hurt and rejected. What are your thoughts about David's outburst of emotion to God?

What conclusions did David come to after exposing his emotions to God (verses 22-23)?

---- ❧ ----

The discipline of emotions is the training of responses.[9]

ELISABETH ELLIOT

8. In Lamentations, Jeremiah also acknowledged his feelings to God. Read Lamentations 3:1-26.

How would you characterize Jeremiah's feelings before verse 21?

What was Jeremiah's *thinking* after verse 21?

This passage reminds us that while it is important to express our feelings, we should not dwell on them but instead exercise our will to think the truth.

Cease to consider your emotions, for they are only the servants; and regard simply your will, which is the real king in your being. Is that given up to God? . . . Does your will decide to believe? Does your will choose to obey? . . . And when you have got hold of this secret . . . that you need not attend to your emotions but simply to the state of your will, all the Scripture commands, to yield yourself to God, to present yourself a living sacrifice to Him, to abide in Christ, to walk in the light, to die to self, become possible to you; for you are conscious that in all these your will can act, and can take God's side; whereas, if it had been your emotions that must do it, you would, knowing them to be utterly uncontrollable, sink down in helpless despair.[10]

HANNAH WHITALL SMITH

DISCIPLINING THE BODY

9. Scripture reminds us that we must honor God with our bodies. Read the following passages, and note the instructions or examples given there.

ROMANS 12:1 ....

1 CORINTHIANS 6:18-20 ·· ↪

1 CORINTHIANS 9:24-27 ······································· ↪

She girds herself with strength [spiritual, mental, and
physical fitness for her God-given task] and makes her
arms strong and firm.

PROVERBS 31:17, AMPC

DISCIPLINING TIME

10. Numerous seminars and books tell us how to manage our
time. But usually we don't need more information—just more
discipline! Read the verses below, and write down what you
learn about using time wisely and why that is important.

PSALM 39:4-5 ·· ↪

11. In her book *Discipline: The Glad Surrender*, Elisabeth Elliot said, "There is always enough time to do the will of God."[11] Would you agree with that statement? Why or why not?

One of Satan's most useful tools is getting us to waste time or to procrastinate. In *The Screwtape Letters*, Screwtape writes his nephew Wormwood about his patient's use of time:

> All the healthy and out-going activities which we
> want him to avoid can be inhibited and *nothing* given
> in return, so that at least he may say, as one of my
> own patients said on his arrival down here, "I now
> see that I spent most of my life in doing *neither* what
> I ought *nor* what I liked."[12]

❦ THOUGHTS AND REFLECTIONS
FROM AN OLDER WOMAN

Certainly excellence in our lives is molded by discipline. Jesus' words are so true: "Keep watching and praying that you may not come into temptation; the spirit is willing, but the flesh is weak" (Mark 14:38). So often my intentions are good, but I'm inconsistent in following through because I don't exercise my will over my feelings or my lazy body! But as Richard Foster once said, "The disciplined person is the person who can do what needs to be done when it needs to be done."[13]

Two cautions concerning discipline: First, *discipline is not rigid*. It does not mean that my schedule can never be interrupted. Foster wrote, "The disciplined person is a flexible person. . . . The disciplined person is always free to respond to every movement of divine Grace."[14] When I am disciplined, I'm usually caught up with my responsibilities and can handle a change of plans and interruptions. It is when I'm behind and undisciplined that I find it hard to be flexible.

The second caution is, *discipline should never become legalistic*. One author defined legalism as "obsessive conformity to a standard for the purpose of exalting self."[15] The purpose of self-discipline is to grow in sound judgment so that we exemplify the character of Christ. Instead of reacting to circumstances, we exercise self-control and respond biblically. We develop the habit of conscientious obedience so that we are available to be used by God and to bring Him glory in all areas of our lives.

I don't want to have regrets at the end of the day because I have been totally undisciplined. I want my focus to be on the Lord and on pleasing Him. This meditation by Joseph Bayly expresses my feelings toward discipline:

> Lord Christ, your servant Martin Luther said he only
> had two days on his calendar: today and "that day."
> And that's what I want too. And I want to live today
> for that day.[16]

PERSONAL THOUGHTS AND REFLECTIONS

12. Hudson Taylor stated, "A man may be consecrated, dedicated, and devoted, but of little value if undisciplined."[17] After studying the different facets of our lives that often need self-control, which area of your life do you feel needs more discipline? Why?

13. What can you do to develop self-control in that area?

14. Consider making a short-term goal for each area we have studied. Use this chart if you find it helpful.

Area	My Goal	Suggested Goals
Mind		Memorize Scripture consistently. Go through a reading plan for the Bible.
Will		Determine what I need to say no or yes to. Cooperate with God in choosing to do what is right.
Emotions		Keep a journal expressing my feelings to God.
Body		Honor God by how I use my body.
Time		Ask God each morning to set my priorities for the day.

SCRIPTURE MEMORY

2 TIMOTHY 1:7—*The Spirit God gave us does not make us timid, but gives us power, love and self-discipline. (NIV)*

CHAPTER 7

Excellence:

GUARDED BY DISCRETION

Discretion will guard you, understanding will watch over you.

PROVERBS 2:11

NOT ONLY DOES DISCRETION—good sense—protect us, but it is also a fundamental aspect of our character. King Solomon said, "A beautiful woman who lacks discretion is like a gold ring in a pig's snout" (Proverbs 11:22, NLT). Solomon might have learned this truth from observing his seven hundred wives and three hundred concubines! Our looks, abilities, and knowledge fade into the background if our behavior does not reflect discretion. Allowing discretion to guard our conduct is vital to becoming a woman of excellence, for a woman who wants to please God by her life will honor Him with gracious, thoughtful speech and actions.

In our last chapter we studied the importance of being molded by discipline and learned that the word *discipline* comes from the Greek word *sōphrōn*. That is the same word that is translated into the word *discretion*. It means to be of sound mind, self-controlled, sane, temperate, and sensible.[1] I think that as I practice self-discipline, it enables me to be discreet—to be careful, sensitive, and godly as I relate to people and my circumstances.

DISCRETION DEFINED

1. Discretion has been defined as saying and doing the right thing in the right way at the right time. To build on this explanation, look up the following words in the dictionary and record their definitions.

   Discreet—

   Discretion—

   Indiscretion—

Prudence—

Sensible—

2. The book of Proverbs teaches us many important truths about wisdom, knowledge, understanding, and discretion. What do you learn about discretion from the following verses?

PROVERBS 2:11 ···

PROVERBS 5:1-2 ···

PROVERBS 8:12 ···

3. In his letter to Titus, the apostle Paul instructed the older women to teach the younger women to be discreet—sensible, temperate, wise. Read Titus 2:3-5. In what important ways can an older woman teach a younger woman to be discreet?

❧ DISCRETION DEMONSTRATED

> Understand this, my dear brothers and sisters: You must all be quick to listen, slow to speak, and slow to get angry. Human anger does not produce the righteousness God desires.
>
> JAMES 1:19-20, NLT

Discretion Is Slow to Speak

4. What do you learn about discretion or indiscretion in the following verses?

PROVERBS 15:28 ⋯⋯⋯⋯⋯⋯⋯⋯⋯⋯⋯⋯⋯⋯⋯⋯⋯⋯⋯⋯⋯⋯⋯

PROVERBS 17:27-28 ⋯⋯⋯⋯⋯⋯⋯⋯⋯⋯⋯⋯⋯⋯⋯⋯⋯⋯⋯⋯⋯

PROVERBS 18:13 ·· ✑

PROVERBS 29:20 ·· ✑

----------------- ✐ -----------------

When I want to speak, let me think first. Is it true? Is it kind? Is it necessary? If not, let it be unsaid.[2]

MALTBIE D. BABCOCK

5. A verse that I often need in my life is Ephesians 4:29. What guidelines did Paul provide in this verse for those who want to be discreet?

———————— ⟨∾⟩ ————————

If I can enjoy a joke at the expense of another; if I can in
any way slight another in conversation, or even in thought,
then I know nothing of Calvary love.[3]

AMY CARMICHAEL

Discretion Is Slow to Anger

6. "A [woman's] discretion makes [her] slow to anger, and it
   is [her] glory to overlook a transgression" (Proverbs 19:11).
   What can you learn from these proverbs about being slow to
   anger?

PROVERBS 12:16 ·· ∾

PROVERBS 15:1 ··· ∾

PROVERBS 16:32 ··· ∾

———————— ⟳ ————————

The key to patience under provocation is to seek to develop God's own trait of being "slow to anger." . . . The best way to develop this slowness to anger is to reflect frequently on the patience of God toward us. The parable of the unmerciful servant (see Matthew 18:21-35) is designed to help us recognize our own need of patience toward others by recognizing the patience of God toward us. . . . We are like the unmerciful servant when we lose our patience under provocation. We ignore God's extreme patience with us. We discipline our children out of anger, while God disciplines us out of love. We are eager to punish the person who provokes us, while God is eager to forgive. We are eager to exercise our authority, while God is eager to exercise His love.

This kind of patience does not ignore the provocations of others; it simply seeks to respond to them in a godly manner.[4]

JERRY BRIDGES

Discretion Dresses Modestly

7. In Romans 12:2 we are told, "Don't copy the behavior and customs of this world" (NLT). In today's culture it is hard to resist the artificial glamour of the world. Study the following passages and record the "dress code" for "women making a claim to godliness" (1 Timothy 2:10).

1 TIMOTHY 2:9-10 ·· ⌒

1 PETER 3:3-4 ·· ⌒

How do these verses speak to your personal life?

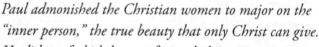

*Paul admonished the Christian women to major on the
"inner person," the true beauty that only Christ can give.
He did not forbid the use of nice clothing or ornaments.
He urged balance and propriety, with the emphasis on
modesty and holy character.*[5]

WARREN WIERSBE

Discretion Plans Ahead

8. Discretion involves the ability to have foresight or to be
   prudent. What do you learn from the following verses about
   "planning ahead"?

PROVERBS 14:15 ·· ᘒ

PROVERBS 31:21 ·· ᘒ

PROVERBS 31:25, 27 ·· ᘒ

BIBLICAL EXAMPLES OF DISCRETION

9. Two biblical women serve as examples of women who were guarded by discretion: Esther and Mary, the mother of Jesus.

   a. Esther was a Jewish woman who was chosen to be the queen of Persia. During her reign, the king's prime minister, Haman, co nvinced the king to sign an edict to destroy all the Jews in the land. Mordecai, Esther's cousin, encouraged her to approach the king about the edict to slaughter the Jews. Read Esther 4:15–5:8 and record your thoughts about how Esther exemplified discretion.

b. Read Luke 2:15-19, and write down your thoughts about how Mary exemplified discretion (v. 19).

❧ THOUGHTS AND REFLECTIONS FROM AN OLDER WOMAN

Discretion is such a need in my life that I have memorized Psalm 69:5-6: "O God, it is You who knows my folly, and my wrongs are not hidden from You. May those who wait for You not be ashamed through me, O Lord GOD of hosts; may those who seek You not be dishonored through me, O God of Israel." These verses are special because I don't want my lack of discretion to dishonor God or be an embarrassment or hindrance to others.

To apply discretion in my life, I have set these goals:

- *Slow to speak*—I pray to remember to think before I speak.
- *Slow to anger*—I pray to be slow to anger not only toward my family but also toward others who frustrate me! (Other drivers, people who wait or don't wait on me in stores, etc.)
- *Dressing discreetly*—I choose not to attract or detract attention by the way I dress. I choose to dress to please God.
- *Planning ahead*—I pray to be faithful in my God-given responsibilities.

Our purpose for being discreet is "that the word of God will not be dishonored" (Titus 2:5). My prayer for you: "May the LORD give you discretion and understanding" (1 Chronicles 22:12, NIV).

❧ PERSONAL THOUGHTS AND REFLECTIONS

10. After studying discretion, how do you think it can guard your life? How can it defend your life, keep you in safety, and hold you secure against objections or attacks?

Applying discretion to our lives brings immediate results. Being slow to speak or slow to anger will become quickly evident to those close to us!

11. What will you do to grow in the area of discretion? What one specific thing will you do to start that growth? (For example: memorize a verse, become accountable to an older woman in the Lord, ask someone's opinion of your dress, get a notebook and begin to plan ahead in order to be faithful in keeping your commitments.)

❧ SCRIPTURE MEMORY

PROVERBS 2:11—*Discretion will guard you, understanding will watch over you.*

Excellence:

MADE PRECIOUS BY A GENTLE AND QUIET SPIRIT

Your beauty should not be dependent on an elaborate coiffure, or on the wearing of jewellery or fine clothes, but on the inner personality—the unfading loveliness of a calm and gentle spirit, a thing very precious in the eyes of God.

I PETER 3:3-4, *Phillips*

A WOMAN WITH A GENTLE and quiet spirit is not only precious to God but also attractive to others. Certainly a hallmark quality of a woman of excellence is a gentle and quiet spirit. That doesn't mean that a gentle and quiet-spirited woman never says anything or never laughs and enjoys life. Instead, she speaks appropriately and wisely. She enjoys life because she is secure and at rest in her spirit. She is gracious, content, and free to give to others.

DEFINING A GENTLE AND QUIET SPIRIT

1. To begin developing an understanding of a gentle and quiet spirit, define the following words:

97

Gentle—

Quiet—

Meek—(The Greek *prays* [meek] and *praytēs* [meekness] are words that consistently convey gentleness, humility, and consideration for others.[1])

Calm—

From your study of these words, write your own definition of a gentle and quiet spirit.

Gentleness

2. In mentoring Timothy, the apostle Paul exhorted him to pursue righteousness, godliness, love, faith, perseverance, and gentleness (1 Timothy 6:11). Why do you think gentleness is included in this list?

3. Peter taught that our beauty is not to be dependent on outward adornment, but to be clothed with inward beauty. Read Colossians 3:12, and write a brief paragraph describing how being clothed in these qualities can produce a gentle spirit.

Quietness

4. Paul wrote to the church at Thessalonica, "Make it your goal to live a quiet life" (1 Thessalonians 4:11, NLT). What do you learn about quietness from the following passages?

PSALM 131 ....

PROVERBS 17:1 .... ✑

ECCLESIASTES 9:17 .... ✑

ISAIAH 30:15 .... ✑

ACQUIRING A GENTLE AND QUIET SPIRIT

5. Jesus described Himself as "gentle and humble" in Matthew
   11:28-30. Read these verses and write down how we should
   respond to His invitation to . . .

"Come"

"Take My yoke"

"Learn from Me"

A quiet time is a time set aside to deepen your knowledge of the Lord, to enrich your own personal relationship with Him, to fellowship with Him, to love Him, to worship Him, on a very personal basis. . . . How much of a calm and gentle spirit you achieve, then, will depend on how regularly and consistently, persistently and obediently you partake of the Word of God, your spiritual food.[2]

SHIRLEY RICE

6. Romans 8:31 states that God is for us and not against us. Knowing that God is on your side can encourage you to rest in Him. In what ways can the following verses about God's care for you help you in acquiring a gentle and quiet spirit?

PSALM 18:30-35

ROMANS 8:28 ·· ꙮ

1 CORINTHIANS 10:13 ····································· ꙮ

---

*We are to desire a richer and more permanent adorning—
that of the heart . . . a calm temper; a contented mind;
a heart free from passion, pride, envy, and irritability; a
soul not subject to the agitations of and vexations of those
who live for fashion, and who seek to be distinguished for
external adorning.[3]*

ALBERT BARNES

7. Being secure in God's loving sovereignty is important for
having a gentle and quiet spirit. Read Ruth 1–2:13.

What in Ruth's life demonstrated that she was placing herself in God's care?

How did God guide and protect her?

Not only does Ruth "just happen" to arrive at Boaz's field but it just so happens that Boaz shows up at the same time. These seeming coincidences reveal the Designer behind the story.[4]

PAUL E. MILLER

KEEPING A GENTLE AND QUIET SPIRIT

8. On the next page is a list of hindrances that keep me from being calm and gentle. You may want to add to the list. Reflect on the following Scripture passages, and write about how you could confront these hindrances in your life. Then use these verses to check yourself when you sense your spirit becoming restless and irritated.

a.   Unconfessed sin—Psalm 32:3-5

b.   Anger—Ephesians 4:26

c.   An unforgiving spirit—Ephesians 4:32

d.   Self-centeredness—Philippians 2:3-4

e.   Anxiety—Philippians 4:6-7

f.   Neglecting responsibilities—Proverbs 31:27

g. Fatigue—Psalm 127:1-2

h. Physical disorders—2 Corinthians 12:7-10

THOUGHTS AND REFLECTIONS
FROM AN OLDER WOMAN

I remember visiting the beautiful home of a friend one day, and that afternoon as I sat in my "less beautiful" home, I did not have a gentle and quiet spirit. As I examined my heart to determine the cause of my frustration, I realized that in my self-centeredness, I was envious, jealous, and discontented with my house. All of these responses are real enemies of maintaining a gentle and quiet spirit!

I become anxious when I get in a hurry or I have overcommitted myself. When I neglect my responsibilities, I begin to become frustrated. When I stay up late and don't get enough rest, it is very hard for me to be kind and gentle. When I do experience disquiet in my spirit, I ask the Lord to show me why I'm that way. As I listen to His thoughts in my heart, I find that most of the time the source of my irritability is one of the hindrances mentioned in the previous pages. Sometimes He has gently reminded me that I have not been spending enough time with Him—for it is in abiding in Christ that the Holy Spirit is able to produce the fruit of gentleness in my life.

My prayer in becoming a woman of excellence is that my focus and energy are centered on inner beauty. I want my responses and conduct to spring from a humble and quiet spirit so that I can be a blessing to those I meet. Certainly excellence is made precious by a gentle and peaceful spirit, but, above all, my desire in acquiring the unfading loveliness of a calm and gentle spirit is that it is very precious in the eyes of God.

I have noticed that wherever there has been a faithful following of the Lord in a consecrated soul, several things have, sooner or later, inevitably followed.

Meekness and quietness of spirit become in time the characteristics of the daily life. A submissive acceptance of the will of God, as it comes in the hourly events of each day, is manifested; pliability in the hands of God to do or to suffer all the good pleasure of His will; sweetness under provocation; calmness in the midst of turmoil and bustle; a yielding to the wishes of others, and an insensibility to slights and affronts; absence of worry or anxiety; deliverance from care and fear,—all these, and many other similar graces, are invariably found to be the natural outward development of that inward life which is hid with Christ in God.[5]

HANNAH WHITALL SMITH

PERSONAL THOUGHTS AND REFLECTIONS

9. Look back over this chapter and write your thoughts about the specific ways you can acquire and keep a gentle and quiet spirit. Then close with prayer and ask God to give you sensitivity to His Spirit when He prompts you to manifest that equanimity of spirit that God so highly esteems.

SCRIPTURE MEMORY

1 PETER 3:3-4—*Your beauty should not be dependent on an elaborate coiffure, or on the wearing of jewellery or fine clothes, but on the inner personality—the unfading loveliness of a calm and gentle spirit, a thing very precious in the eyes of God. (Phillips)*

Excellence:

PERFECTED BY PURITY

Like the Holy One who called you, be holy yourselves also in all your behavior; because it is written, "YOU SHALL BE HOLY, FOR I AM HOLY."

I PETER 1:15-16

TO KNOW, EXPERIENCE, OR SEE God has been the deep desire and longing of all who truly love Him. As the apostle Paul wrote, "I count all things to be loss in view of the surpassing value of knowing Christ Jesus my Lord" (Philippians 3:8). In the Sermon on the Mount, Jesus taught that those who are pure in heart will see God (Matthew 5:8). Certainly we will see God in glory, but here on earth the pure in heart can "see mysteries of grace, mysteries of love and holiness which are hidden from the eyes of the unclean."[1]

To be holy is to be morally blameless, to be separated from sin and therefore consecrated to God. "God has provided all we need for our pursuit of holiness," wrote Jerry Bridges. "He has delivered us from the reign of sin and given us His indwelling Holy Spirit. He has revealed His will for holy living in His Word, and He works in us to will and to act according to His good purpose."[2] Our challenge today is being pure in such an unprincipled generation! What help and encouragement can we receive from the Scriptures in our goal of perfecting excellence through purity?

🌿 GOD'S DESIRE FOR PURITY

1. Oswald Chambers stated, "There is a danger of forgetting that the Bible reveals, not first the love of God, but the intense, blazing holiness of God, with his love as the center of that holiness."[3] What do you learn about God's holiness from the following verses?

PSALM 99:3, 5, 9 ···

ISAIAH 6:1-4 ··

HEBREWS 7:26 ···

REVELATION 4:8 ·······································

2. Ephesians 5:1 instructs us, "Be imitators of God, as beloved children." God desires that we bear an increasing resemblance to Himself. From each of the following passages, list the truths that seem most significant to you as you become an "imitator" of God's holiness and purity.

EPHESIANS 5:1-4 ·······································

1 THESSALONIANS 4:3-8 ·······························

HEBREWS 12:14 ·······································

1 PETER 1:13-16 ·······································

———————— ✦ ————————

Holiness is a dull word these days, conjuring up images of fusty finger-wagging prigs, who are good in the worst sense of the word, men and women with sullen, morose faces, full of rectitude and rigid duty, "on hold for the next life," as a Washington Post *writer once put it.*

True holiness, however, is anything but dull. It is startling and arresting. It's more than being decent, good, ethical, and upright. It has that aspect the Bible calls, "the beauty of holiness."[4]

DAVID ROPER

GOD'S DESIGN FOR PURITY

3. In the New Living Translation, Hebrews 12:14 says, "Work at living in peace with everyone, and work at living a holy life." It does take work to choose to be holy. What are the major battlefields or stumbling blocks we face in our goal of living a holy and pure life?

MARK 7:15, 20-23 ·····································

EPHESIANS 6:10-12 ·····································

1 CORINTHIANS 6:18-20 ···

JAMES 1:13-16 ··

1 JOHN 2:15-16 ··

As you examine your life, on which battlefield do you most often find yourself?

———— ⌒ ————

How does a child of God go about overcoming the desires of the old nature? He must begin each day by yielding his body to God as a living sacrifice (Rom. 12:1). He must spend time reading and studying the Word of God, "feeding" his new nature. He must take time to pray, asking God to fill him with the Holy Spirit and give him power to serve Christ and glorify Him.

As he goes through the day, a believer must depend on the power of the Sprit in the inner man. When temptations come, he must immediately turn to Christ for victory.[5]

WARREN WIERSBE

4. Romans 6:6 tells us, "We know that our old sinful selves were crucified with Christ so that sin might lose its power in our lives. We are no longer slaves to sin" (NLT). What do you learn about rejecting sin from the following verses?

ROMANS 6:11-14 ....

COLOSSIANS 3:1-5 ....

1 JOHN 3:7-9 ....

Elisabeth Elliot commented on the characteristics of the old nature as they are described in Colossians 3:5:

> *These are the* products *of human desire, if human desire is given free reign. The Christian has handed the reins over to his Master. His human desires are brought into line. The desires still exist, are still strong, natural, and human, but they are subjugated to the higher power of the Spirit. They are purified and corrected as we live day by day in faith and obedience.*[6]

5. In dealing with temptation, the Bible tells us to make a specific response not only to God but also to Satan or to our old nature. Look up the following verses, and write the desired response in the appropriate column.

Verses	Response to God	Response to Satan or old self
Ephesians 6:10-11	Put on the full armor of God	Stand firm against the devil's schemes
Colossians 3:9-10		

James 4:7		
1 Peter 5:8-9		

---

*To experience joy, we must make some choices. We must
choose to forsake sin, not only because it is defeating to us,
but because it grieves the heart of God. We must choose
to count on the fact that we are dead to sin, freed from
its reign and dominion, and we can now actually say
no to sin. We must choose to accept our responsibility to
discipline our lives for obedience.*[7]

JERRY BRIDGES

6. A. W. Tozer observed, "Long practice in the art of mental
   prayer (that is, talking to God inwardly as we work or travel)
   will help to form the habit of holy thought."[8] As we commit
   to purity, we must understand the importance of guarding
   our hearts and our thoughts. What do you learn from the
   following passages about establishing holy thinking?

PSALM 119:9-11 ···

PHILIPPIANS 4:8 ··· ᘒ

7. It is important to be fully aware of the sin around you and to also be assured that "greater is He who is in you than he who is in the world" (1 John 4:4). What can you discover from the following verses about how to be perfected by purity?

PROVERBS 4:23 ··· ᘒ

GALATIANS 5:16-18 ··· ᘒ

2 PETER 1:3-4 ··· ᘒ

---------------- ✑ ----------------

If there is an Enemy of Souls (and I have not the slightest doubt that there is), one thing he cannot abide is the desire for purity. Hence a man or woman's passions become his battleground. The Lover of Souls does not prevent this. I was perplexed because it seemed to me He should prevent it, but He doesn't. He wants us to learn to use our weapons.[9]

ELISABETH ELLIOT

8. Many years ago I realized that I must have convictions about various facets of purity in my life. Pray about, think over, and write down what decisions you can make to demonstrate purity in the following areas:

Your relationships with men:

Your dress:

Your speech:

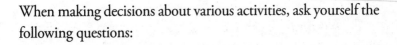

Your activities:

When making decisions about various activities, ask yourself the following questions:

Is it helpful—physically, spiritually, and mentally? (See 1 Corinthians 6:12.)

Does it bring me under its power? (See 1 Corinthians 6:12.)

Does it hurt others? (See 1 Corinthians 8:13.)

Does it glorify God? (See 1 Corinthians 10:31.)

Can I do it in Christ's name? (See Colossians 3:17.)

Wheresoever we be, whatsoever we are doing, in all our work, in our busy daily life . . . He is with us, and all we do is spread before Him. Do it, then, as to the Lord. Let the thought of His eye unseen be the motive of your acts and words. Do nothing you would not have Him see. Say nothing which you would not have said before His visible presence. This is to do all in His name.[10]

HENRY EDWARD MANNING

GOD'S DELIGHT IN PURITY

9. Paul wrote to Timothy that "he has saved us and called us to a holy life—not because of anything we have done but because of his own purpose and grace. This grace was given us in Christ Jesus before the beginning of time" (2 Timothy 1:9, NIV). Since God has called us with a holy calling, what are the blessings of living a pure life?

PSALM 24:3-6 ....

MATTHEW 5:8 ···

1 JOHN 3:2-3 ···

——————————— ༄ ———————————

*It is quite true to say—"I cannot live a holy life," but you
can decide to let Jesus Christ make you holy.*[11]

OSWALD CHAMBERS

THOUGHTS AND REFLECTIONS
FROM AN OLDER WOMAN

Over the years of pursuing purity in my life, I discovered a very
helpful explanation of sin, which Susanna Wesley expressed in
a letter to her son John. Her definition of sin has guided me
and helped me immensely, especially in the "gray" areas. Sin is
"whatever weakens your reason, impairs the tenderness of your
conscience, obscures your sense of God, or takes off the relish of
spiritual things . . . that thing is sin to you, however innocent it
may be in itself."[12]

So many things can challenge my desire to be holy—what I

watch, what I listen to, what I read. It takes determination and discernment to not compromise my pursuit of purity.

Certainly not all novels, media, and music are impure. Paul wrote in 1 Corinthians 6:12, "As a Christian I may do anything, but that does not mean that everything is good for me. I may do everything, but I must not be a slave of anything" (*Phillips*). The question for the committed Christian is this: How will this book or form of entertainment influence my walk with God and my thought life?

Another aspect of purity that I have to evaluate constantly is the subtlety of compromise and comparison. Often I think, *Well, at least I don't do that*, or *I'm not as bad as many others*, or *My little sins are nothing compared to what she does!* The thought that helps me is that I should not compare my purity to others' purity but to Christ's purity. Jesus said, "I always do the things that are pleasing to Him" (John 8:29).

The best way for me to fulfill my calling to be holy in all my behavior is to consistently abide in Christ. It is the one discipline that has helped me to guard my heart and to be fully armored. Cherishing His Word with a heart to obey is a proven way of walking in the Spirit. Staying connected to Christ keeps me from *practicing* sin, from habitually sinning. It's not that I don't sin; I do. But if I am abiding in Christ, I am sensitive to any sin I commit and to the Holy Spirit's promptings to confess my sin and be forgiven. My closeness to Christ determines my sensitivity to sin. Nineteenth-century Bible scholar Thomas D. Bernard's thoughts are so true: "Our sense of sin is in proportion to our nearness to God."[13]

I am always challenged by the woman of excellence described

in Proverbs 31:10: "Who can find a virtuous woman? for her price is far above rubies" (Proverbs 31:10, KJV).

🌿 PERSONAL THOUGHTS AND REFLECTIONS

Some precious words of an old hymn tell us that God's grace is greater than all our sin. Perhaps there has been some impurity in your past. The Scriptures state, "If we confess our sins, He is faithful and righteous to forgive us our sins and to cleanse us from all unrighteousness" (1 John 1:9). Our confession brings cleansing.

If you want to remain pure, make an effort to have friends who practice purity. To help in areas of vulnerability, it is good to have someone you can call or go to for special prayer.

10. Write out a prayer to God expressing your desire to live a holy and pure life. You might want to include some thoughts from this old hymn:

> *More purity give me,*
> *More strength to o'er-come;*
> *More freedom from earth-stains,*
> *More longings for home;*
> *More fit for the Kingdom,*
> *More useful I'd be;*
> *More blessed and holy;*
> *More, Savior, like Thee.*[14]

"MORE HOLINESS GIVE ME," PHILIP P. BLISS

MY PRAYER TO BE PERFECTED BY PURITY:

 ## SCRIPTURE MEMORY

1 PETER 1:15-16—*Like the Holy One who called you, be holy yourselves also in all your behavior; because it is written, "YOU SHALL BE HOLY, FOR I AM HOLY."*

Excellence:

PROCLAIMED BY WISDOM

The wisdom from above is first pure, then peaceable, gentle, reasonable,
full of mercy and good fruits, unwavering, without hypocrisy.

JAMES 3:17

THE BOOK OF JAMES gives us a beautiful description of wisdom
in James 3:17. His definition could be a good summation of our
study of excellence. Wisdom, as we will be studying, "depends on
right conduct in obedience to the will of God rather than theoretical insight."[1]

The word translated "wise" comes from the Greek word *sophos*,
which describes "one with moral insight and skill in the practical
issues of life."[2] Proverbs 4:7 says, "Getting wisdom is the wisest
thing you can do!" (NLT). If we are to become women of excellence, we must pursue wisdom. It's the wise thing to do.

ESSENTIALS OF WISDOM

1. After Daniel was delivered from his night in the lion's den,
   King Darius made this declaration: "I decree that everyone

throughout my kingdom should tremble with fear before the God of Daniel" (Daniel 6:26, NLT). The king understood the foundational requirement for acquiring wisdom. What further insight can we find in the following passages?

JOB 28:28 ·· ❧

PROVERBS 9:10 ·· ❧

PROVERBS 15:33 ·· ❧

---·····❧·····---

Fearing the Lord means having a deep reverence and respect for God and His Word, a respect and reverence that result in obedience.[3]

BILL HAMMER

2. In his letter to the Corinthian church Paul wrote, "To those who are the called, both Jews and Greeks, Christ [is] the power

of God and the wisdom of God" (1 Corinthians 1:24). What truth is communicated in the following verses?

1 CORINTHIANS 1:30 ···

COLOSSIANS 2:2-3 ···

3. Warren Wiersbe categorized the qualities of wisdom as "man-made wisdom" and "heavenly wisdom."[4]

   a. Read James 3:13-18, and in the appropriate columns write down the various aspects of worldly wisdom and heavenly wisdom. (You might find it helpful to read the passage in several translations.)

Worldly Wisdom	Heavenly Wisdom

b. After contemplating these lists, write a brief evaluation of how wisdom is manifested in your life.

Lord,
Open my ears!
So much of what I read in your Word speaks
of the importance of hearing.
Wisdom demands it;
Righteousness requires it;
Understanding necessitates it.
I see so much of selective hearing.
Am I a selective listener?
Do I only hear what I want to?
Oh, Father!
You know I long to be
wise,
understanding,
discerning. . . .
Teach me to open my ears and
really hear.[5]

CAROLE MAYHALL

ACQUIRING WISDOM

4. Proverbs 22:17 encourages us to "listen to the words of the wise" (NLT). Clearly, heartfelt listening is a valuable way to acquire wisdom. What additional ways of obtaining wisdom can you learn from these verses?

PROVERBS 2:1-10 ....

PROVERBS 13:20 ....

MATTHEW 7:24-25 ....

JAMES 1:5-6 ....

--- ❦ ---

We must "ask" for wisdom. Then and only then can it be given. "Wisdom," wrote Spurgeon, "is a beauty of life that can only be produced by God's workmanship in us."

God is not satisfied to save us from this world alone. He wants to change us, to make us real in the righteousness that is in His Son. The only path to real change is to ask for His help. When we do, we're in for the full treatment. God's goal for us is greater than we could ever imagine.[6]

DAVID ROPER

❧ CHARACTERISTICS OF WISDOM

5. James 3:13 instructs us, "Who is wise and understanding among you? Let them show it by their good life, by deeds done in the humility that comes from wisdom" (NIV). Read the following passages and answer these two questions about each verse:

- *What is my need in this area?*

- *What can I do to grow in the kind of behavior that shows wisdom and understanding?*

PROVERBS 9:8 .... ❧

PROVERBS 10:8 ···

PROVERBS 12:18 ···

PROVERBS 15:31 ···

PROVERBS 29:11 ···

————— ⁀ —————

*The chief means for attaining wisdom, and suitable gifts
for ministry, are the Holy Scriptures and prayer.*[7]

JOHN NEWTON

BENEFITS OF WISDOM

6. Wisdom is not without its benefits and blessings. Read the following verses and list the fruit of wisdom.

PROVERBS 3:13-18 ....

PROVERBS 8:10-11 ....

PROVERBS 8:32-35 ....

THOUGHTS AND REFLECTIONS FROM AN OLDER WOMAN

Wisdom is living life in an excellent way—the way God intends for us to live. I am passionate about learning truth from Scripture, for Jesus taught that when we listen and obey His teachings, we are wise. The key to His teaching in Matthew 7, though, is His emphasis on not just hearing the Word but also living it out in our everyday life. I've always thought that wisdom and knowledge were somewhat equal. While knowledge of God is a necessary component in acquiring wisdom, it is in *applying* knowledge to my life that makes me wise. It is what makes us authentic Christians.

In his book *Growing Slowly Wise*, David Roper shared this insight: "It's not what we *know* that makes us wise, but what we *are*. James makes that very clear: 'Let the wise man show his wisdom by his *good life*, by deeds done in the humility that comes from wisdom.' Wisdom is the 'good life,' or, more precisely, the 'beautiful life'—a holy, genial presence that makes visible the life of our invisible Lord."[8]

I am challenged by the qualities of wisdom listed in James 3:17: pure, peace loving, gentle at all times, willing to yield to others, full of mercy and good deeds, shows no favoritism, and is always sincere (NLT). The *Amplified Bible* (Classic Edition) version of this passage adds the words *courteous* and *considerate* to the word *peace-loving*. Roper noted that "the text actually reads, 'Let him show forth his deeds in gentle wisdom.'"[9] I like that. The life of a woman of excellence is proclaimed by her gentle wisdom.

When looking back on the lives of men and women of God, the tendency is to say, "What wonderfully astute wisdom they had! How perfectly they understood all God wanted!" The astute mind behind them is the Mind of God, not human wisdom at all. We give credit to human wisdom when we should give credit to the Divine guidance of God

through childlike people who were foolish enough to trust
God's wisdom and the supernatural equipment of God.[10]

OSWALD CHAMBERS

❧ PERSONAL THOUGHTS AND REFLECTIONS

7. What the world calls wisdom and what the Word calls wisdom
   are two different things. James 3:13-18 describes wisdom in
   terms of our character. Reread the passage, and write why you
   think these qualities are given to describe wisdom.

8. Proverbs 4:13 urges us to "take hold of my instructions; don't
   let them go. Guard them, for they are the key to life" (NLT).
   As you review this chapter and consider the Scripture passages
   you have studied, write your strengths and weaknesses in
   acquiring wisdom.

9. Prayerfully record the ways you can begin to grow in wisdom.

Never walk away from Wisdom—she guards your life;
love her—she keeps her eye on you.
Above all and before all, do this: Get Wisdom!
Write this at the top of your list: Get Understanding!
Throw your arms around her—believe me, you won't regret it;
never let her go—she'll make your life glorious.
She'll garland your life with grace,
she'll festoon your days with beauty.

PROVERBS 4:6-9, MSG

 ## SCRIPTURE MEMORY

JAMES 3:17—*The wisdom from above is first pure, then peaceable,*
gentle, reasonable, full of mercy and good fruits, unwavering,
without hypocrisy.

PART FOUR

The Praise

CHAPTER 11

Excellence:

PORTRAYED IN THE LIFE
OF A GODLY WOMAN

*Charm is deceptive, and beauty does not last; but a woman who fears
the LORD will be greatly praised.*

PROVERBS 31:30, NLT

I HOPE THAT as you have studied *Becoming a Woman of Excellence*,
you have sensed that our lives are precious to God, so precious that
He has given us specific guidelines to keep our hearts pure and
open before Him. In a beautiful "last act" in His book on wisdom,
God draws a portrait of a woman who epitomizes excellence.

The book of Proverbs begins with this declaration: "Fear of
the LORD is the foundation of true knowledge, but fools despise
wisdom and discipline" (Proverbs 1:7, NLT). And Proverbs ends with
this truth: "Charm is deceptive, and beauty does not last; but a
woman who fears the LORD will be greatly praised" (Proverbs 31:30,
NLT). "So we come back to the maxim with which the whole book
began, that the foundation of all excellence is the fear of the Lord."[1]

The essence of the woman described in Proverbs 31 was her reverence and awe of God. Several ways she exemplified excellence were by her commitment to God, her graciousness, her discretion, her diligence, her trustworthiness, and her wisdom.

Speaking of this praiseworthy woman, Derek Kidner wrote, "Her charm and her success . . . owe nothing to chance, because her outlook . . . and her influence . . . have the solid foundation of the fear and wisdom of the Lord."[2] Truly this woman is an example of one whose goal was to honor God and pursue excellence.

❧ A PATTERN OF EXCELLENCE

1. Read Proverbs 31:10-31. In the space provided after the corresponding verses, write down the character qualities that motivated the woman to do what she did. Although the woman described in Proverbs 31 was married, the spiritual qualities of her life speak to all women, whether married or single. If you are single, in place of "husband" and "children" in these verses, you can substitute family or friends. Ask yourself, *Whose heart is trusting me? Whom am I committed to serve and minister to?*

PROVERBS 31:11-15 ·

PROVERBS 31:16-20 ·

PROVERBS 31:21-24 ··· ⌒

PROVERBS 31:25-27 ··· ⌒

PROVERBS 31:28-31 ··· ⌒

2. After reflecting on these character qualities, summarize the characteristics and attributes that you consider to be indispensable in becoming a woman of excellence.

✿ THOUGHTS AND REFLECTIONS FROM AN OLDER WOMAN

The woman described in Proverbs 31 has been my mentor for many years. I have learned from her wholehearted example of living out her everyday life for God. The priority in this woman's life is seen in verse 30—her fear of God. It is her spiritual life that is commended and is the cornerstone of her excellence. Her example has deeply influenced my desire to seek the Kingdom of God above all else.

As I have studied and meditated on Proverbs 31, I think that I discovered one of the secrets of this woman's excellence: she realized that only she could be responsible for her life. Her choices, responses, and her walk with God were solely her responsibility; only she could give an account of her life to God.

Goals and desires are not the same. Larry Crabb has noted that the difference between a goal and a desire is whether we can or cannot control the situation.[3]

If I want to lose weight, I can make that a legitimate goal, because I am the one responsible for what I eat and whether I exercise. However, if I want a friend or loved one to lose weight, that can only be a desire because I cannot control his or her eating or exercising! There is nothing wrong with desires, but it is very important to discern the difference between what I can and cannot control in life. A goal is something that I can be totally responsible for; I do not have to depend on anyone else to get that goal accomplished.

In a friendship or marriage, I cannot have a *goal* of having a good friendship or marriage because that involves someone else. However, I can *desire* to have a good relationship. As such I can pray and cooperate in the relationship to make it so. A proper goal for me in a friendship is to be a good friend and in marriage to be a good wife because that is something I can control.

I think that the woman described in Proverbs 31 is a model for taking responsibility for our part in living a godly life. The chapter is full of *she* does, *she* seeks, *she* is, *she* brings, *she* stretches, *she* speaks.

It is good to examine our responses in different situations to see if we are trying to control or manipulate someone else. Richard

Foster has written, "We must come to the place in our lives where we lay down the everlasting burden of needing to manage others."[4] To become a woman of excellence, I just need to manage myself! The apostle Peter reminds us, "Remember that the heavenly Father to whom you pray has no favorites. He will judge or reward you according to what you do. So you must live in reverent fear of him during your time here as 'temporary residents'" (1 Peter 1:17, NLT).

My becoming an excellent woman is not dependent on anyone else: it is dependent on my decision to be God's woman who fears Him, who derives her worth and security from Christ, and who is then free to serve and love others to His glory.

Proverbs 31:30-31 tells us that "charm is deceptive, and beauty does not last; but a woman who fears the LORD will be greatly praised. Reward her for all she has done. Let her deeds publicly declare her praise" (NLT). The woman described in Proverbs 31 was praised first by her husband and family, which is evidence that she lived her priorities and that her deeds were an affirmation of her character to the world.

Earlier in this study we looked at Ruth's excellent life, and it is special to read that after her marriage to Boaz, she gave birth to her son, Obed. Naomi's friends rejoiced, and we find in Ruth 4:15 their tribute to Ruth: "He is the son of your daughter-in-law who loves you and has been better to you than seven sons!" (NLT). This is very high praise for Ruth and is a testimony of her life of excellence.

The ultimate praise we seek, though, is from the Lord. I believe that only as I set my heart to follow hard after Him, to become a woman whom He can use, to be excellent in all I do, will I receive His praise. How I long to hear the Lord say, "Well done, my good and faithful woman of excellence."

Thus is shut up this looking-glass for ladies, which they are desired to open and dress themselves by; and if they do so, their adorning will be found to praise and honour, and glory, at the appearing of Jesus Christ.[5]

MATTHEW HENRY

 PERSONAL THOUGHTS AND REFLECTIONS

Now that you have completed your study, let me briefly summarize the chapters.

If our *goal* is to become women of excellence, we must "approve the things that are excellent" and seek to become like Christ.

The *cost* of becoming a woman of excellence involves surrendering our lives and obeying God's commands. That is the way He intends for us to live.

The *prize* or reward that we receive in pursuing excellence is that we will be molded by discipline, guarded by discretion, made precious by a gentle and quiet spirit, perfected by purity, and filled with heavenly wisdom.

If we "add" these qualities to our lives, then we will portray a woman who reverences God and who receives praise.

3. As you reflect on all you have learned about excellence, take time to carefully review your study and note any special insights and applications you have made. Then prayerfully record your summation of a woman of excellence, concluding

with specific guidelines you feel you need to keep you on your journey of becoming a woman of excellence.

Personal Goals

Paul stated his personal goal in 2 Corinthians 5:9: "We make it our goal to please him" (NIV). I would like to share the goal I have set for my life: "My goal is to honor the Lord in my thoughts, speech, actions, and activities by approving those things that are excellent; to exemplify Christ's character as I respond to people and circumstances; and to continually deepen my fellowship and knowledge of God and His Word."

One of the life goals that has shaped me through the years is the goal of Betty Scott Stam. Betty and her husband, John, were missionaries to China in the early 1940s. The 1949 Chinese Communist Revolution culminated in the party's take-over of China. During this "War of Liberation," both Betty and her husband were beheaded for their faith. Betty's goal has challenged me and many others to become women of excellence, women whose reverence for God impels them to willingly give their lives to be used by Him for the fulfillment of His purposes:

> Lord, I give up all my own plans and purposes, all my own desires and hopes, and accept Thy will for my life. I give myself, my life, my all utterly to Thee to be Thine forever. Fill me and seal me with Thy Holy Spirit. Use me as Thou wilt, send me where Thou wilt, work out Thy whole will in my life at any cost, now and forever.[6]

My goal is God Himself, not joy nor peace, nor even blessing, but Himself, my God.
'Tis His to lead me there, not mine but His.
"At any cost, dear Lord, by any road!"[7]

FRANCES BROOK

4. In the first chapter of our study, you were asked to write a personal goal as you began your journey of excellence. After studying many aspects of excellence and now understanding the difference between a goal and a desire, perhaps you would like to revise your goal at this time. When you have prayerfully considered this goal, I encourage you to write it in the front of your Bible so that you can be reminded of your commitment to God.

MY PERSONAL GOAL:

 SCRIPTURE MEMORY

PROVERBS 31:30—*Charm is deceptive, and beauty does not last; but a woman who fears the LORD will be greatly praised.* (NLT)

Now that you have finished this study, I encourage you to take a block of time and memorize Proverbs 31:10-31. It has been a blessing to me, and the Lord has used many of these verses to encourage me at special times.

the Father spoke:

Are you ready to continue our journey, My child?

Yes. Although I have much more to learn, I now have my heart set
to approve those things that are excellent.

*It is enough that your intent is to become excellent. As long as you
abide, I will continue to teach you and transform you into the
image of My Son.*

Thank You, Father. I want all that You desire for me.

*Come, keep your hand in Mine and become a woman of excellence
who brings Me glory.*

I hold you by your right hand—
I, the LORD your God.
And I say to you,
"Don't be afraid. I am here to help you."

ISAIAH 41:13, NLT

A Guide

FOR BIBLE STUDY LEADERS

AS YOU LEAD YOUR GROUP, keep in mind the purpose of this study: to motivate a pursuit of excellence in our Christian pilgrimage, to realize that this pursuit is a lifelong process, and to learn to make specific applications of the Scriptures to our lives. A wholehearted approach to applying what is learned should produce growth and change. I hope that when you finish the study, your group will not be the same as when you began! Your group purpose should be to provide insights, challenges, accountability, and prayer support for one another.

If you opt to use the first meeting as an introductory time, you might want to follow this suggested outline:

1. Have each member introduce herself and tell about her family and her Christian experience.

2. Pass out the study books, and look together at the format of the study. Note the table of contents, quotations from Christian writers, author's reflections, personal applications, and Scripture memory passage.

3. Explain that the Scripture memory verse for each lesson is found at the beginning and end of each chapter. Encourage group members to write the verse on a 3" x 5" card or a Post-it note, using their favorite Bible translation, and then place the verse somewhere where they will see it every day. You can divide the group into pairs so that at each meeting, the two people can recite the memory verse to each other.

4. As a group, you might want to set standards for your time together. These standards could include the commitment to attend the study, to memorize the Scripture verses, to complete the homework for each chapter, and to apply the study with diligence.

5. Talk with the group about having prayer partners during the study. These partners would not have to meet together outside of the group sessions, but they could share requests during the week.

6. At the end of your meeting, pray and ask the Holy Spirit to speak to each woman's heart during the weeks of the study.

When you meet together later as a group to discuss the chapters of this study, you might use this structure:

1. Begin each session by asking the women to share their key thoughts, new insights, or questions about the topics raised by the subheadings in the chapters.

2. Invite women to share how they were able to apply the Scripture passages and new insights to their personal lives.

3. Spend some time with the Scripture memory passage, asking women to recite it to each other.

4. Pray together, asking women to pray aloud, if they are comfortable. If your group has prayer partners, these women could spend a few minutes together, sharing answers to prayer and praying for each other.

To prepare yourself for the group experience, consider these activities:

1. Pray—for the Holy Spirit to guide the women as they study, for the individual women in your group, for wisdom and grace for yourself as you lead the group.

2. As you study before each meeting, you might also want to prepare specific questions for each section. You will find additional information and clarification in commentaries, a Bible dictionary, or other resources. Of course, your greatest resource is sensitivity to the Holy Spirit as He guides and directs the study according to the needs of the group.

About the Author

CYNTHIA HALL HEALD is a native Texan. She and her husband, Jack, a veterinarian by profession, are on staff with The Navigators in Tucson, Arizona. They have four children—Melinda, Daryl, Shelly, and Michael—as well as eleven grandchildren.

Cynthia graduated from the University of Texas with a BA in English. She frequently speaks to church women's seminars and conferences, both nationally and internationally.

She loves to be with her family, share the Word of God, have tea parties, and eat out.

BIBLE STUDIES, BOOKS, VIDEOS, AND AUDIOS
by Cynthia Heald

BIBLE STUDIES:
Becoming a Woman of Excellence
Becoming a Woman of Faith
Becoming a Woman of Freedom
Becoming a Woman of Grace
Becoming a Woman of Prayer
Becoming a Woman of Purpose
Becoming a Woman of Simplicity
Becoming a Woman of Strength
Becoming a Woman Who Loves
Becoming a Woman Whose God Is Enough
Intimacy with God
Walking Together (adapted from *Loving Your Husband* and *Loving Your Wife* by Jack
    and Cynthia Heald)

BOOKS AND DEVOTIONALS:
Becoming a Woman Who Walks with God (a gold-medallion-winning devotional)
Drawing Near to the Heart of God
Dwelling in His Presence
I Have Loved You
Maybe God Is Right After All
Uncommon Beauty
Promises to God

VIDEO DOWNLOADS AND DVDs OF THE FOLLOWING STUDY ARE AVAILABLE AT CYNTHIAHEALD.COM:
Becoming a Woman Whose God Is Enough

VIDEO DVDs OF THE FOLLOWING STUDIES ARE AVAILABLE FROM NAVPRESS:
Becoming a Woman of Simplicity
Becoming a Woman of Strength

AUDIO DOWNLOADS OF THE FOLLOWING STUDIES ARE AVAILABLE AT CYNTHIAHEALD.COM:
Becoming a Woman of Simplicity
Becoming a Woman of Strength
Becoming a Woman Whose God Is Enough

Notes

CHAPTER 1—EXCELLENCE: A GOAL WORTH PURSUING
1. Charles Colson, *Loving God* (Grand Rapids, MI: Zondervan, 1984), 14.
2. David Atkinson, *The Message of Ruth* (Downers Grove, IL: InterVarsity Press, 1985), 49–50.
3. Oswald Chambers, quoted in *The Quotable Oswald Chambers*, compiled and edited by David McCasland (Grand Rapids, MI: Discovery House, 2008), 89.
4. Charles R. Swindoll, *Growing Strong in the Seasons of Life* (Portland: Multnomah, 1983), 53.

CHAPTER 2—EXCELLENCE: GOD'S CHARACTER
1. A. W. Tozer, *The Knowledge of the Holy* (San Francisco: Harper & Row, 1961), 123.
2. Tozer, *The Knowledge of the Holy*, 24.
3. Alexander Maclaren, in *The Westminster Collection of Christian Quotations*, compiled by Martin H. Manser (Louisville, KY: Westminster, 2001), 137.
4. Amy Carmichael, *If* (Fort Washington, PA: CLC Publications, 2012), 27.
5. Tozer, *The Knowledge of the Holy*, 115.
6. Eugene Peterson, *A Long Obedience in the Same Direction* (Downer's Grove, IL: InterVarsity Press, 1980, 2000), 42–43.
7. Tozer, *The Knowledge of the Holy*, 69.
8. Charles Haddon Spurgeon, *The Sword and the Trowel*, (London: Passmore & Alabaster, 1866), 550.
9. George Mueller, quoted in *Streams in the Desert*, compiled by L. B. Cowman, edited by Jim Reimann (Grand Rapids, MI: Zondervan, 1997), 37.
10. Oswald Chambers, quoted in *The Quotable Oswald Chambers*, compiled and edited by David McCasland (Grand Rapids, MI: Discovery House, 2008), 157.

CHAPTER 3—EXCELLENCE: BECOMING LIKE CHRIST

1. Eugene Peterson, *A Long Obedience in the Same Direction* (Downers Grove: InterVarsity Press, 1980, 2000), 16.
2. Oswald Chambers, *My Utmost for His Highest* (New York: Dodd, Mead & Co., 1966), February 8.
3. Oswald Chambers, *The Place of Help*, quoted in *The Quotable Oswald Chambers*, compiled and edited by David McCasland (Grand Rapids, MI: Discovery House, 2008), 187.
4. Andrew Murray, *Abide in Christ* (Springdale, PA.: Whitaker House, 1980), 5.
5. Ibid., 7, 15.
6. Dwight L. Moody, quoted in *The Westminster Collection of Christian Quotations*, compiled by Martin H. Manser (Louisville, KY: Westminster, 2001), 23.
7. William Carey, quoted in Richard Foster, *Prayer* (New York: HarperCollins, 1992), 57.
8. Charles Haddon Spurgeon, *Treasury of David* (London: Passmore & Alabaster, 1872), 134.
9. Chambers, *My Utmost for His Highest*, November 30.
10. Tim Kenny, "Steps to Peace with God," Billy Graham Evangelistic Association, September 23, 2004, http://billygraham.org/decision-magazine/october-2004/steps-to-peace-with-god/.
11. "The Bridge to Life," The Navigators, January 31, 2006, https://www.navigators.org/Tools/Evangelism%20Resources/Tools/The%20Bridge%20to%20Life.
12. "Got 7 Minutes for God?" The Navigators, October 1, 2012, http://www.navigators.org/Tools/Newsletters/Featured%20Newsletters/Disciple/October%202012/October%202012/Got%207%20Minutes%20for%20God.

CHAPTER 4—EXCELLENCE: ROOTED IN SURRENDER

1. François Fénelon, *Let Go* (Springdale, PA.: Whitaker House, 1973), 6.
2. Oswald Chambers, *My Utmost for His Highest* (New York: Dodd, Mead & Co., 1966), October 23.
3. Richard Foster, *Celebration of Discipline* (New York: HarperCollins, 1978, 1998), 112.
4. Bill Hull, *Jesus Christ, Disciplemaker* (Colorado Springs: NavPress, 1984), 170.
5. Hannah Whitall Smith, *The Christian's Secret of a Happy Life* (Westwood, NJ: Revell, 1888), 54–55.
6. Chambers, *My Utmost for His Highest*, December 24.
7. Lydia Joel, quoted in *Parade* magazine, August 22, 1982.
8. C. S. Lewis, *The Screwtape Letters* (New York: HarperCollins, 2015), 65.
9. A. W. Tozer, *The Pursuit of God* (Harrisburg, PN.: Christian Publications, Inc., 1948), 23.
10. Elisabeth Eliot, *Discipline* (Grand Rapids, MI: Revell, 2006), 116.
11. François Fénelon, *The Best of Fenelon*, "The Death of Self" (Gainesville, FL: Bridge-Logos Publishers, 2002), 10.

12. George Mueller, quoted in Simon Guillebaud, *More Than Conquerors: A Call to Radical Discipleship* (Oxford, UK: Monarch Books, 2009), 103.
13. Chambers, *My Utmost for His Highest*, April 12.
14. Whitall Smith, *The Christian's Secret of a Happy Life*, 39.

CHAPTER 5—EXCELLENCE: EXEMPLIFIED BY OBEDIENCE
1. Hannah Whitall Smith, *The Christian's Secret of a Happy Life* (Westwood, NJ: Revell, 1888), 202.
2. Edward B. Pusey, *Parochial Sermons* (Oxford: James Parker & Co., 1868), 346.
3. John Flavell, quoted in Charles Haddon Spurgeon, *The Treasury of David* (New York: Funk and Wagnalls, 1885), 276.
4. C. S. Lewis, *The Screwtape Letters* (New York: HarperCollins, 2015), 67.
5. *Roget's Thesaurus in Dictionary Form*, edited by Norman Lewis, s.v. "deceive."
6. Oswald Chambers, *My Utmost for His Highest* (New York: Dodd, Mead & Co., 1966), November 2.
7. Amy Carmichael, *Thou Givest . . . They Gather* (Ft. Washington, PA: Christian Literature Crusade with Dohnavur Fellowship, 1958), 114.
8. *The Bible Knowledge Commentary*, edited by John F. Walvoord and Roy B. Zuck (Wheaton: Victor Books, 1983), 27.
9. Ibid., 820.
10. Warren Wiersbe, *The Wiersbe Bible Commentary: New Testament* (Colorado Springs, CO: David C Cook, 2007), 851.
11. L. B. Cowman, comp., *Streams in the Desert*, edited by Jim Reimann (Grand Rapids, MI: Zondervan, 1997), July 19, 267.
12. Charles R. Swindoll, *Growing Strong in the Seasons of Life* (Grand Rapids, MI: Zondervan, 1983), 146.
13. Thomas Carter in *Joy and Strength*, compiled by Mary W. Tileston (New York: Grosset & Dunlap, 1929), March 25.

CHAPTER 6—EXCELLENCE: MOLDED BY DISCIPLINE
1. *Webster's Ninth New Collegiate Dictionary* (Springfield, MA: Merriam-Webster Inc., 1988), s.v. "discipline."
2. Warren Wiersbe, *The Wiersbe Bible Commentary: New Testament* (Colorado Springs, CO: David C. Cook, 2007), 773.
3. Oswald Chambers, *My Utmost for His Highest* (New York: Dodd, Mead & Co., 1966), May 10.
4. *The New International Dictionary of New Testament Theology*, edited by Colin Brown, vol. 3 (Grand Rapids, MI: Zondervan, 1971), 502, 494, 496, 313.
5. Richard Foster, "And We Can Live By It: Discipline," *Decision Magazine*, September 1982, 11.

6. "Mind" in *New International Dictionary of New Testament Theology*, edited by Colin Brown, vol. 3 (Grand Rapids, MI: Zondervan, 1976), 617.

7. Hannah Whitall Smith, *The Christian's Secret of a Happy Life* (Westwood, NJ: Revell, 1888), 80.

8. Larry Crabb, *Basic Principles of Biblical Counseling* (Grand Rapids, MI: Zondervan, 1975), 47.

9. Elisabeth Elliot, *Discipline: The Glad Surrender* (Old Tappan, NJ: Fleming H. Revell, 1982, 2006), 145.

10. Whitall Smith, *The Christian's Secret of a Happy Life*, 84–85.

11. Elliot, *Discipline*, 99.

12. C. S. Lewis, *The Screwtape Letters* (New York: HarperCollins, 2015), 60.

13. Foster, "And We Can Live By It: Discipline," 10.

14. Ibid.

15. Michael A. Straessle, *Is There Really a Purpose?* (Bloomington, IN: AuthorHouse, 2004), 10.

16. Joseph Bayly, *Psalms of My Life* (Carol Stream, IL: Tyndale, 1969), 42.

17. Dr. and Mrs. Howard Taylor, *Hudson Taylor in Early Years: The Growth of a Soul* (New York: Hodder & Stoughton, 1912), 46.

CHAPTER 7—EXCELLENCE: GUARDED BY DISCRETION

1. *The Analytical Greek Lexicon Revised*, edited by Harold K. Moulton (Grand Rapids, MI: Zondervan, 1978), 396.

2. Maltie D. Babcock, quoted in *Worth Repeating*, edited by Bob Kelly (Grand Rapids, MI: Kregel Publications, 2003), 319.

3. Amy Carmichael, *If* (Fort Washington, PA: CLC Publications, 2012), 15.

4. Jerry Bridges, *The Practice of Godliness* (Colorado Springs: NavPress, 1983), 207–208.

5. Warren Wiersbe, *The Wiersbe Bible Commentary: New Testament* (Colorado Springs, CO: David C. Cook, 2007), 746.

CHAPTER 8—EXCELLENCE: MADE PRECIOUS BY A GENTLE AND QUIET SPIRIT

1. William Klein, "Greek Word Study," *The Small Group Letter*, vol. 1, no. 2, May 1984, 6.

2. Shirley Rice, *The Christian Home: A Woman's View* (Norfolk, VA: Norfolk Christian Schools, 1965).

3. Albert Barnes, *Notes Explanatory and Practical on the General Epistles of James, Peter, John and Jude* (London: Knight and Son, 1854), 201.

4. Paul E. Miller, *A Loving Life* (Wheaton, IL: Crossway, 2014), 77.

5. Hannah Whitall Smith, *The Christian's Secret of a Happy Life* (Westwood, N.J.: Fleming H. Revell, 1888), 203–204.

CHAPTER 9—EXCELLENCE: PERFECTED BY PURITY

1. B. C. Caffin, *The Pulpit* Commentary, edited by H. D. M. Spence and Joseph S. Excell, vol. XV, Matthew (Peabody, MA: Hendrickson, 1985), 174.
2. Jerry Bridges, *The Pursuit of Holiness* (Colorado Springs, CO: NavPress, 1984), 157.
3. Oswald Chambers, quoted in *The Westminster Collection of Christian Quotations*, compiled by Martin H. Manser (Louisville, KY: Westminster, 2001), 132.
4. David Roper, *Growing Slowly Wise* (Grand Rapids, MI: Discovery House, 2000), 9.
5. Warren Wiersbe, *The Wiersbe Bible Commentary: New Testament* (Colorado Springs, CO: David C. Cook, 2007), 987.
6. Elisabeth Elliot, *Passion and Purity* (Old Tappan, NJ: Revell, 1984), 94.
7. Bridges, *The Pursuit of Holiness*, 157.
8. A. W. Tozer, *The Price of Neglect and Other Essays* (Camp Hill, PA: Christian Publications, 1991), 110.
9. Elliot, *Passion and Purity*, 26.
10. Henry Edward Manning, *Joy and Strength*, selected by Mary W. Tileston (New York: Grosset & Dunlap, 1929), December 23.
11. Oswald Chambers, *My Utmost for His Highest* (New York: Dodd, Mead & Co., 1966), July 9.
12. Susanna Wesley, quoted in John Whitehead, *Rev. John Wesley* (Boston: Dow & Jackson, 1845), 222.
13. Thomas D. Bernard, quoted in Gordon S. Jackson, *Quotes for the Journey, Wisdom for the Way* (Colorado Springs: NavPress, 2000), 154.
14. Philip P. Bliss, "More Holiness Give Me" (1873).

CHAPTER 10—EXCELLENCE: PROCLAIMED BY WISDOM

1. *The New International Dictionary of New Testament Theology*, edited by Colin Brown, vol. 3 (Grand Rapids, MI: Zondervan, 1971), 1028.
2. *The Bible Knowledge Commentary*, ed. John F. Walvoord & Roy B. Zuck (Wheaton: Victor Books, 1983), 828.
3. Bill Hammer, "Take a Drink from the Fountain of Wisdom," *Discipleship Journal* 2.5 (September 1982), 8.
4. Warren Wiersbe, *The Wiersbe Bible Commentary: New Testament* (Colorado Springs, CO: David C. Cook, 2007), 870.
5. Carole Mayhall, *Lord, Teach Me Wisdom* (Colorado Springs: NavPress, 1979), 48–49.
6. David Roper, *Growing Slowly Wise* (Grand Rapids, MI: Discovery House, 2000), 38.
7. John Newton, *The Works of the Rev. John Newton* (New York: Robert Carter, 1847), 115.
8. Roper, *Growing Slowly Wise*, 112.
9. Ibid., 115.
10. Chambers, *My Utmost for His Highest* (New York: Dodd, Mead & Co., 1966), October 26.

CHAPTER 11—EXCELLENCE: PORTRAYED IN THE LIFE OF A GODLY WOMAN

1. W. J. Deane and S. T. Taylor-Taswell, in *The Pulpit Commentary*, edited by H. D. M. Spence and Joseph S. Excell, vol. IX, Proverbs (Peabody, MA: Hendrickson, 1985), 602.

2. Derek Kidner, *Proverbs: An Introduction and Commentary*, Tyndale Old Testament Commentaries (Downers Grove, IL: InterVarsity, 1975), 184.

3. Larry Crabb, *The Marriage Builder* (Grand Rapids, MI: Zondervan, 1982, 1992), 74–75.

4. Richard Foster, *Celebration of Discipline* (New York: HarperCollins, 1978, 1998), 10.

5. Matthew Henry, *Matthew Henry's Commentary on the Whole Bible*, vol. 3 (Iowa Falls, IA: Riverside Book and Bible House, n.d.), 977.

6. Betty Scott Stam, quoted in Elisabeth Elliot, *Let Me Be a Woman* (Carol Stream, IL: 1976), viii.

7. Frances Brook, "I Follow After," *The Weekly Evangel*, 172 (January 13, 1917), 1.

Become the Woman God Created You to Be

978-1-60006-663-4
DVD 978-1-61521-821-9

978-1-57683-831-0

978-1-63146-564-2

978-1-61521-023-7

978-1-61521-021-3

A goal worth pursuing. Society beckons us to succeed—to achieve excellence in our appearance, our earning power, our family life. God Himself also beckons us to be women of excellence. But what exactly is He asking? If you're hungry for God's perspective on success, dig into God's Word with bestselling Bible teacher Cynthia Heald and experience the joy of becoming a woman of excellence.

Becoming a Woman of Grace
978-1-61521-022-0

Becoming a Woman of Strength
978-1-61521-620-8 | DVD 978-1-61747-902-1

Becoming a Woman of Freedom
978-1-57683-829-7

Becoming a Woman of Prayer
978-1-57683-830-3

Becoming a Woman Whose God Is Enough
978-1-61291-634-7

A NavPress resource published in alliance
with Tyndale House Publishers, Inc.

Available wherever books are sold.

CP0794